LEGO with DAD

**Creatively Awesome
Brick Projects** for
Parents and Kids to
Build **Together**

Warren Nash

rockynook

Lego with Dad:
Creatively Awesome Brick Projects for Parents and Kids to Build Together
Warren Nash

Editor: Kelly Reed
Project manager: Lisa Brazieal
Marketing coordinator: Mercedes Murray
Copyeditor: Linda Laflamme
Proofreader: Stephanie Argy
Interior design: Aren Straiger
Composition: Kim Scott, Bumpy Design
Cover production: Aren Straiger
Cover photograph: Warren Nash

ISBN: 978-168198-586-2
1st Edition (1st printing, October 2020)
© 2020 Warren Nash
All photographs © Warren Nash

Rocky Nook Inc.
1010 B Street, Suite 350
San Rafael, CA 94901
USA
www.rockynook.com

Distributed in the UK and Europe by Publishers Group UK
Distributed in the U.S. and all other territories by Ingram Publisher Services

Library of Congress Control Number: 2019950817

This book is printed on acid-free paper.
Printed in Korea.

Dedicated to my awesome little man, Charlie,
and my wife, Trisha,
for supporting me every step of the way.

CONTENTS

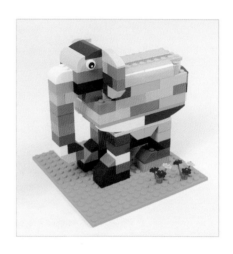

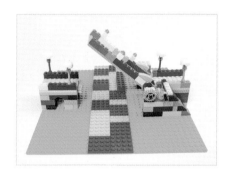

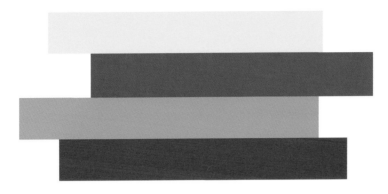

Introduction

Hi, I'm Warren, and I'm a dad! I've been creating videos on YouTube for about five years now, focusing mainly on DIY and food. Since the birth of my son, however, I've spent more time producing videos based around fatherhood, creative tasks, and educational games you can get your kids involved in. And, of course, some of these involve LEGO!

I've been passionate about LEGO all my life. I began playing with LEGO at a really young age, and it has grown with me, keeping my imagination and creativity alive into adulthood.

Remember, LEGO isn't just for kids. It's okay for us adults to play with it at our age too!

Building Bonds

Now, my son is showing an interest in everything, and I'm keen to show other families fun ways to strengthen their bonds with something that has played such a big role in my life growing up: LEGO. With all that in mind, I thought the time was finally right to publish a book that includes all the LEGO builds I've loved as a kid and an adult. The builds are perfect for people of all ages to create together, and now they're all here in one place.

As you'll see, *LEGO with Dad* demonstrates how building with LEGO can strengthen family bonds through collaborative play and problem-solving. The book includes a library of LEGO builds for all skill sets, as well as essential LEGO hints and tips. Each LEGO build has simple steps and a multitude of in-progress images, making the process easy to follow for parents and children alike. Whether you're looking to build something big or small, something that moves, or something you can give as a gift, you'll find it here.

Although you can certainly bounce around the book to try projects in the order they interest you and your family, the builds do get progressively more complicated in later chapters. If you're new to building, Chapter 3's classics will help you warm up and hone your skills. On the other hand, if you're looking for ways to add a new dimension to your builds, Chapter 6 will show you how to add gears and motion while challenging your building skills.

Every moment shared between children and their parents is one to be cherished. It's a dream come true that I'm publishing *LEGO with Dad*, because writing it brought back so many memories of building with my father. Maybe that special LEGO helper in your family is Mom, a grandparent, or an older sibling; no matter who it is, I hope the builds you find in the following pages inspire you to keep creating. My goal is to demonstrate how much value creating masterpieces together can bring to your families.

Finding Time for Creative Play

I know: Even simple masterpieces take time, and time can be hard to find. With so much going on, simply getting through the day can be a real achievement sometimes! As a parent, I feel guilty if I struggle to fit a decent amount of playtime into the day, and for me, it's always important to mix playtime up as much as possible. That's why LEGO is such a brilliant toy. When you're struggling to find something new for your kids to do, give them a box of LEGO and some building ideas. It's amazing how long they'll stay occupied.

One thing I've learned as a parent is the importance of planning ahead. For example, if you anticipate being out and about with your family, whether for a long stretch or just daily errands, why not bring LEGO with you? My Maze and Alphabet games (Chapter 3) make great on-the-road projects. LEGO is not a toy that has to be confined to your home; it's also just as brilliant to play with in the car or on holiday.

For my son, I created a little LEGO travel box. While the adults are packing all the vacation essentials, the kids can get involved packing as many bricks as they want to bring, as long as they fit in the box! Likewise, if you're busy in the yard in the summer, bring LEGO outside. It's just as much of an outdoor toy as an indoor toy. Plus, if you lay it out on a picnic blanket, you can easily pack all the LEGO away by wrapping up the picnic blanket.

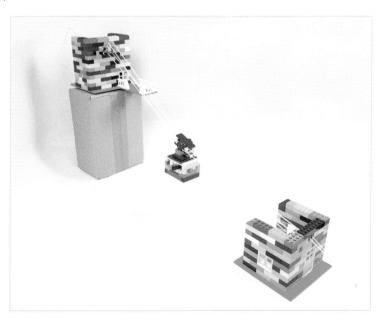

For complex builds, such as my Crane (Chapter 5) or Cable Car (Chapter 6), make a plan to tackle the project over multiple sessions—giving you and your child something to look forward to each evening for a week. Or, divide up the project: While you handle work or chores, your child can complete a piece, then you both incorporate it into the larger build together once you're free—or vice versa!

The great thing about LEGO is the more you play with it, the more you'll see the opportunities it brings. Once you and your family get the bug, you'll more easily spot chances in the day to enjoy creative play. Whether it's for just 10 minutes on the go or keeping busy for an entire day, LEGO really is the *best* toy to keep the entire family occupied.

Why LEGO?

In the eyes of a kid, LEGO is constantly reinventing itself. Unlike other toys, as a child grows, their imagination develops, and they learn more at school, LEGO grows with them. That, to me, is the number one reason why I feel LEGO is simply the best toy out there. And hey, it has certainly stood the test of time, which must say something!

It's so easy to get bored of modern-day toys, whereas LEGO always changes. You use the same building blocks, but the challenges you set yourself make LEGO different every time you play with it. As time goes on, those challenges get harder, which means your kids' minds are constantly developing as they discover new ways to be more intuitive, imaginative, and successful master LEGO builders.

Remember, there are no limits. That's why this book is just as much for adults as it is for kids. From the simplest to the most complex builds, we really can build whatever we want from the humble LEGO brick. The more you play with LEGO, the more you'll love it and the more creations you'll make from it. So, let's go forth and be the best LEGO builders we can be!

1

Essential Materials

Which Sets Should I Get?

When creating the builds for this book, I relied on the Large Creative Brick Box (10698) and Bricks on a Roll (10715) set. Set 10698 is a great starter set that has all the essential bricks you'll need, including small baseplates. Set 10715 includes more moving pieces, which is perfect for transport and moving builds. I found one lot of this set was enough to accomplish everything I wanted. The majority of bricks used in the book's builds come from these sets. I used two 10698s, in part because its small baseplates are so useful, and one 10715. To supplement these sets, it's also worth getting at least one large baseplate—or more if you like to keep your creations on display or plan to give them as gifts. Large baseplates are available in a range of colors, so you can easily simulate grass, water or even a concrete jungle!

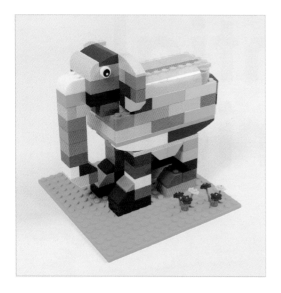 

As a fan of moving Lego builds, I also recommend you consider buying a LEGO motor. Although you can certainly add motion manually with gears and cranks, a motor can really help to bring builds alive, as you'll see in Chapter 6.

That said, let me stress that you don't have to buy new sets to create the following chapters' builds. Delve into your old box of LEGO, and you may be surprised what you find. (If you're like me, you'll probably find your childhood sets have a lot of teeth marks in them!) It's always useful to keep hold of your old LEGO bricks, as you never know when you'll need them again. The more you have, the more you can build!

The 10 Most Useful Bricks

When building with LEGO, you'll find there are some staple bricks you'll always rely on and be constantly searching for. Here are the top 10 essential bricks I just can't live without!

2x4 Brick

Patented by LEGO on January 28, 1958, the 2x4 brick is by far the most essential brick you'll need. Throughout the book, I call this brick a *regular* or *basic brick* because it's height is the standard upon which other bricks are proportionally scaled. For example, the height of 3 plate bricks is the height of one basic brick, as explained further in chapter 2.

You'll struggle to build anything without using this LEGO staple, so make sure you have plenty!

1x6 Brick

Well, it doesn't really matter how long they are to be honest. All regular-height x1 bricks are super useful. Because they're narrow, they're great to fill in gaps as well as providing the sides for containers and so on.

4x1x1 Bow Brick

Bow bricks are handy to give your LEGO builds a nice finishing touch. I'm always using them on the side of roofs or anywhere a corner could benefit from a curved edge.

Knob Brick

Knob bricks are great for adding extra detail in lots of different places. For example, you can use them to add lights or antennas to builds as embellishments. Most bricks will fit onto these so the possibilities are endless.

Roof Tile Brick

Adding a bit of a slope to your builds, roof tile bricks (or simply *tile* bricks) are essential if you need a less blocky look. You can put these to work in lots of different places—from roofs to car hoods to animals and more.

Inverted Roof Tile Brick

Inverted roof tile bricks are similar to roof tile bricks, but upside down! These are great if you need a sloping effect on the underside of your build, such as underneath an airplane.

Baseplates

Why use a baseplate under your build? Ever try to build a tall, narrow tower on a thick carpet? I have, which is why I now build so many of my constructions on something to keep them steady. A decent sized baseplate also gives you space to add embellishments around your main structure to help bring it to life.

Wheels

Did you know LEGO is the biggest manufacturer of tires in the world? Whether they're for an airplane, a car, or something more unusual, you'll always find a use for LEGO tires with a rim inside. Just make sure you have a rim element brick so you can attach your wheels to your build. Plus, the rims alone can be useful to double as pulley, train wheels, and more.

Plate Bricks

Plate bricks come in all different sizes and have lots of different uses. Three stacked on top of each other equals the height of one regular brick. In addition, they're great for building flat roofs or a small base to support a structure on.

Element Separator

Although not a brick, an element separator is such a useful tool that I always keep by my side. With an element separator, you can easily take bricks apart from each other. I find one especially useful when trying to extract those pesky plate bricks!

Brick and Building Resources

As your builds get more ambitions, you may find you need a super-specific brick or need more of one type than your sets include. One option to consider is purchasing a set that includes one or more of the bricks you're looking for; you'll also benefit from all the extra pieces. Alternatively, you can buy specific bricks individually. Most official LEGO stores and LEGOLAND parks feature a Pick A Brick station where you can fill a cup with all the bricks you need—kid in a candy shop time! You can also order individual bricks from the LEGO website's Pick A Brick page (lego.com/page/static/pick-a-brick). If you don't know a brick's official name, you can use a number of filters to narrow your search down.

BrickLink (bricklink.com) is another really useful site. Not only is it an online encyclopedia for new and old LEGO bricks, you can also purchase and exchange LEGO pieces there, including those that are no longer being manufactured. It's a great source of information and has an active community behind it.

If ever you're in need of more inspiration or need to know the best way to build something, you can find a number of resources online. For example, the Lego Access channel on YouTube includes builds you can follow along with, as well as lots of LEGO news, such as the latest set launches. The official LEGO site (lego.com) has loads of useful information on it too. I enjoy the Ideas page (ideas.lego.com), where you'll find lots of LEGO builds submitted by people from around the world. You can browse through photos and vote for your favorites—all while gathering inspiration for your own builds.

With your bricks in hand, you're probably ready to get building. You could jump straight to the projects in Chapter 3 and beyond. If you're new to building, however, Chapter 2 offers some tips and techniques to help you make sturdier structures, more efficient gear assemblies, and more!

FAMILY SPOTLIGHT

Parents: Jen and Jesse Salucci
Location: Belmont, MA
Kids: Rocco (5.5 years old) and Matteo
(2 years old—does more smashing than
building at this point!)

What are your kid's favorite projects to build?
Rocco loves to build vehicles, boats, and
BattleBots (robots that battle). He especially likes
to make items with hidden compartments or
functioning weapons (such as BattleBot flippers or
smashing/punching hammers, powered by rubber
bands).

What do you enjoy most about building with your child?
I love watching him explore unusual or novel ways to use the pieces. Sometimes he comes up with
configurations that I never would have thought of myself!

Do you usually keep your projects together or break them down afterwards?
We keep them intact until at least the weekend, and we take photos of them on Saturday mornings.
So far, we have about 300 documented.

Do you and/or your kids have a dream LEGO project they'd like to build?
His dream is to build a giant tank with a rocket launcher on the top. Ideally, it would be
remote-controlled!

2

LEGO How-tos

If you're like me, you want your LEGO creations to be as spectacular as possible, as well as structurally sound. Through years of creating things with LEGO, I've learned that the finer details are what bring my builds to life. Whether it's something you've quickly put together or a creation you've spent all day on, there are lots of nice little touches that can really help make a build more interesting and further inspire creativity. I've also learned that using certain building techniques will help keep your creation in one piece! This chapter covers just a few of these techniques, which you can use in loads of different ways. I hope you find them useful and inspirational.

Structural Basics

It's likely that one of the first things you built with LEGO involved building a wall. Ensuring your walls are structurally sound is really important, especially as your build progresses and your wall starts to support more and more of your structure.

To make your wall secure, always step back each course by one half brick. For example, if your first layer of bricks uses 2x4 pieces, you should start the next layer with one 2x2 brick. Then, revert back to starting with a 2x4 brick on the third layer. Repeat this process to the top of your wall, and use the same technique when working around obstacles such as doors and windows.

This is a traditional bricklaying technique that goes back centuries and is still a fundamental building technique to this day. Because it ensures the seams between bricks never stack directly on top on one another, this method helps your walls stay together as one and stand more securely—just like in my House build in Chapter 4.

It's also worth remembering that the height of a plate brick is one-third the height of a standard LEGO brick. So, if you need to insert a holder into a wall, such as a plate brick with a clip or hole, you'll need two additional plate bricks along with the holder to keep the courses of your wall level.

When building with LEGO, it's always important to have the end goal in mind throughout the entire build process. This way, you can be confident your builds will be structurally sound for their purpose. For example, when designing my Crane build (Chapter 5), I had to ensure the weight of the boom and anything it was lifting would be balanced by a counterweight at the other end. Similarly, if you try the Bookends build in Chapter 4, think about the books you'll be using them with. To support the weight of the books, the size of each bookend needs to be large enough, and you may need extra supports in place at the front of each bookend so they don't collapse under the weight of books leaning up against them. What's sturdy holding a few paperbacks, may not be hardy enough to brace several oversize picture books.

Unusual Brick Combinations

It's okay if you and your child struggle for inspiration when building with LEGO. Luckily, making things from LEGO doesn't have to be a case of just placing one brick on top of another. For instance, you can attach plate bricks to other bricks in unusual combinations to make your build even more unique.

Suppose your LEGO build requires a track, like in Chapter 4's Railway Station build. Try combining plate bricks together as shown to create one. It's a great way to add movement to your build using simple LEGO pieces and bypasses the need for actual track. You can use this technique to create all kinds of structures to make your build even cooler, while encouraging your kids to think outside the box.

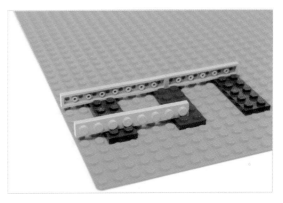

Similarly, did you know if you line up rows of knob bricks, you can attach bricks onto the sides of these? This technique has many useful applications. In Chapter 3, you'll use it to attach a radiator grille and lights to the front of a car, for example, or you can even use it to attach LEGO bricks sideways onto a structure.

Why not add a 1x1 knob brick to the side of your structure and attach a LEGO minifigure rappelling down the side?

Remember, a lot of the time if bricks fit together in unusual ways, it's by design. So as long as your structure remains secure, roll with it and see how unusual brick combinations can enhance your LEGO build.

Enhancing Your Builds with Decorative Pieces

Sometimes when you and your family have spent the time to build something, it just requires that extra little something to finish it off. Luckily, loads of LEGO pieces and brick combos can give your creation the finishing touches it needs. Plus, adding embellishments is a brilliant way to get your children to think about all the little things that contribute to a build and its function. Decorative pieces make your creation even more fun to engage with, so why wouldn't you add a few finishing touches? I'm still discovering new ways to add decoration to my builds.

Embellishments

An easy way to bring a house to life is by adding classic LEGO pieces such as flowers, trees, and fences. Flowers and trees provide a bright boost of color, as well as contribute to a flourishing garden. Whether your house is set in an exotic location or leafy suburbs, there are loads of different variants to choose from to make a house fit right in.

You can keep unwanted neighbors out of your new garden with some fencing. In addition, LEGO fences are handy for creating boundaries and balconies when building architectural pieces. Don't overlook them for other types of builds, either. Trains, cars, and other forms of transport all benefit from fencing to provide safety barriers for passengers.

Lighting

Give your LEGO house that extra bit of sparkle with some lighting. You can use 1x1 round plate pieces with many other LEGO bricks to create lampposts, spotlights, and more. For my house, I incorporated 1x2 plate pieces with a shaft into the brickwork to make angled spotlights.

Need a lamppost instead? Check out the Bridge build in Chapter 5. It incorporates simple lampposts built with "final" bricks, antenna bricks, and small orange nose cone bricks.

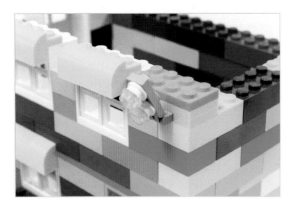 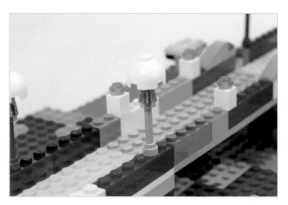

Using Curved Pieces

Sometimes the blocky look just won't do, which is why having a selection of curved bricks at hand is always a good idea. Various types of curved bricks can give your LEGO build the finishing touches it needs. A great example of this is the Elephant build in Chapter 5: 4x1x1 bow bricks make the elephant's body rounded at the top, while long reverse bow bricks mimic a rounded belly and 1x3 bow bricks top the ears. You'll also use a 2x3 arch brick for the top of the trunk and more curved bricks for the head.

LEGO in Motion: Using Gears

I love LEGO creations that include some form of movement, and I bet your kids will too! If your build incorporates spinning pieces (whether turned manually or with a motor), you may find you need to increase or decrease the speed of the moving parts. Building a simple set of gears can help control the speed of your spinning element, and it's a fun introduction to physics for your child.

To build a basic gear, place two cogs of different sizes beside each other—one on an axle and one on the element you want to spin. The size of the cog on the axle providing motion determines whether your spinning element will spin slower or faster than the speed of the motion source.

Here are three gear examples that you can easily incorporate into any LEGO build.

High Gear

Things going a bit too slow for you? Putting together a high gear will speed them up. Suppose you're spinning an axle by hand, but you can't do so fast enough to get your spinning element to turn at the rate you'd like. In this case, a gear that has a larger cog on the axle providing the turning force is required. Next to this, another axle with a significantly smaller cog is needed.

Check out the examples here. While the larger cog will turn more slowly, it does so with more force. Due to the difference in size of the cogs, this force will spin the smaller cog faster, increasing the speed of the second axle.

A basic gear like this is more suitable when the turning force is provided by hand, such as in my Helicopter build (Chapter 6). Why not get your kids to see if they can notice the difference in speed?

Low Gear

At the other end of the spectrum, if your turning force is super-fast, because you're using a LEGO motor for example, you may need the speed of your spinning element to be slower than the motor.

The principles are exactly the same as when creating a high gear, but reversed. In this case, apply the small cog to the axle attached to your motor and attach the large cog to the axle with your spinning element, as shown.

If you don't have a motor with different speed settings, then this is the gear you need.

Worm Gear

A LEGO worm gear does the same job as a low gear: It slows down a turning force. However, the speed difference is much greater with this type of gear. As you can see, the screw-like gear (the *worm*) attaches to your spinning axle and a cog attaches to the element you want to turn.

Interestingly, this type of gear cannot be reversed; using a cog on the axle of your turning force cannot spin a worm gear to increase the speed of your second axle.

This is the technique you will use for the Cable Car build (Chapter 6) to ensure the car travels up the cableway at a smooth, steady pace.

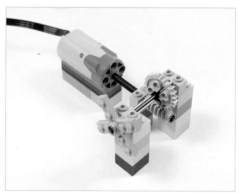

Changing the direction of axles

There may often be times where you need to change the route a driving force is taking. For example, you may have a spinning axle that needs to turn a corner in order for it to function how you expect.

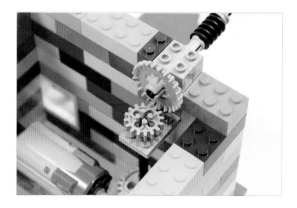

This can be easily achieved by aligning two cogs at a 90 degree angle from each other, where the teeth of the 2 cogs interlink. x1 wide bricks with holes in will help you achieve this, and this method is used in a number of the builds in Chapter 6—LEGO in motion.

Keep Experimenting

The techniques in this chapter are just a preview of some of the useful tips you'll learn in this book to enhance your LEGO builds. If you'd like to practice specific skills, here are a few projects to check out. My Airport Control Tower (Chapter 4) and Wind Turbine (Chapter 6) builds are great for honing your wall-building skills. Whereas if you want to add lots of decoration, my Nightlight (Chapter 3) and Gas Station (Chapter 5) builds are perfect. Interested in messing around with gears? Check out Chapter 6 to explore LEGO creations with moving parts.

You'll also find, with time, you'll teach yourselves loads of clever little hacks to enhance your creations. Think of the tips in this chapter as stepping stones on your journey.

FAMILY SPOTLIGHT

Parent: Jake Flaherty
Location: Albany, CA
Kid: Owen Flaherty, age 8 at the time of the build

What are your kid's favorite projects to build?
Castles, forts, and zoos.

What do you enjoy most about building with your child?
What I enjoy most about building with Lego with my son is how projects evolve. We start with a basic idea of a structure and we talk about what we could do this time. Every build is part of a series of builds. Over time we experiment and try new things. The most excitement comes from the question of "what shall we do this time."

Do you usually keep your projects together or break them down afterwards?
Our builds stay up for weeks or months, but eventually get broken down for new builds.

Do you and/or your kids have a dream LEGO project they'd like to build?
We have not built anything for a few years now (he's almost 13). Our last build was our biggest; a fort with a jail and a garden.

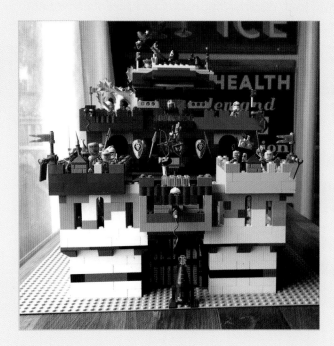

3

Classic Creations

From various modes of transport to animals to games to a night-light, these are some of my all-time classic LEGO builds. Not only will they help jump-start your family's creative juices when you're struggling for inspiration, they also demonstrate some of the cool things you can build with more basic LEGO bricks.

Remember, you don't have to stick to the directions exactly. If you're building a car and your son's working on a boat, why not combine the two to create an amphibicar? You like the giraffe project, but your daughter wants to build something with wings? I've always wondered what a flying giraffe would look like—maybe she could show us!

LEGO creations don't have to be elaborate to be memorable. Sometimes simple projects like these can create the best and most lasting family memories, simply because you enjoy the time creating together.

Car

Specialty pieces needed:

- Steering wheel
- Windshield
- 1x1 plate brick with holder
- Mini antenna

My son is *obsessed* with cars. If your kids are too, then building one from LEGO should be at the top of your list. Plus, because cars come in all kinds of shapes and sizes, creating one can really trigger your kid's imagination.

Making a car can be as simple as attaching some wheels and a steering wheel to a small baseplate. You've probably tried that version already, however, so I'm going to show you how to make a LEGO car that's a little bit more special, using all kinds of quirky bricks you may have struggled to decide what to do with before. Just remember, these steps are just a starting point. Your car can be whatever you want it to be—whether it has 10 wheels or wings on the side, every LEGO car is special!

STEP 1

Find a baseplate to form the chassis of your car. Don't let size limit you either, go as big or small as you want, depending on what type of car you want to build.

STEP 2

To the underside of the baseplate, add a smaller baseplate or plate bricks. Onto this second plate, add some standard 2x2 and 2x4 bricks. You'll be attaching the wheels to these next.

STEP 3

Onto the bricks on the underside of your car, attach two 2x4 wheel suspension bricks (these are what the wheels will attach to). Also attach some 1x2 inverted roof tile bricks around where the wheels will sit. To ensure the roof tile bricks don't rub against them, decide what size wheels you'll be using and check that they fit.

STEP 4

A car needs brake lights, so add some 1x1 knob bricks along with some red light bricks to the back of the car. (Or, leave these off and hope your kid doesn't build a police car to catch you.)

STEP 5

Start to build up the sides of the car by using x1 and x2 wide regular bricks along the edge and back of the car's chassis, leaving some room at the front for the hood and lights.

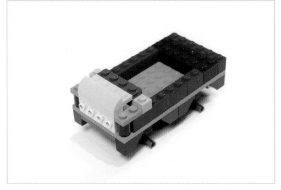

STEP 6

For the front, use a row of knob bricks for the grille and lights, along with various other bricks. To give the hood a nice curved effect, fix a 4x1x1 bow brick in place just above the grille.

STEP 7

Now add some finishing touches to the front, including a radiator grille brick, some light pieces and 1x3 bow bricks for the sides of the hood.

STEP 8

Don't forget to include a steering wheel!

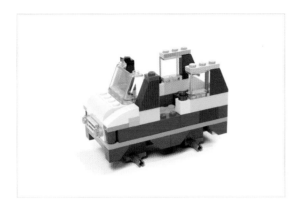

STEP 9

Finish building up all sides of the car with another layer of bricks and tall roof tile bricks. Also add a windshield to the front of the car, as well as windows at the rear so passengers can see out.

STEP 10

When you're happy all sides of the car are level with each other, place a small baseplate brick on top of the car for the roof. Also, why not add some accessories to your car, such as a radio antenna?

STEP 11

To complete your car, place all four wheels onto the wheel suspension bricks on the underside of the car. Take it for a spin!

Forest Tree

Specialty pieces needed:

- Flowers

Walks through the park in the town where I grew up inspired this LEGO build. Tall trees with squirrels jumping between them made me realize how cool a big LEGO forest tree could look. This build has a quirky rugged trunk and little details to bring it to life.

The structural properties of LEGO means you don't have to stick to a strict symmetrical shape when building with it. This build goes for something a little more asymmetrical to make the tree look even more realistic.

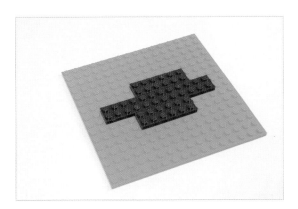

STEP 1

Find a green baseplate, and then attach some brown plate bricks. These plate bricks are the roots of the tree, which you'll build the trunk on.

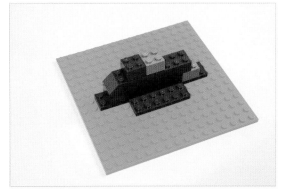

STEP 2

Using basic LEGO bricks and regular and inverted roof tile bricks, start building up the trunk of the tree. Use bricks of varying shades of brown, and build them up in a random, "non-straight" way to help make the trunk look more natural.

STEP 3

When you've made the tree trunk as tall as you want it, start adding various shades of green LEGO bricks.

STEP 4

Within the green bricks, try adding some 1x2 colored bricks to give the tree a bit of color. Are these fruits of the forest, blossoms, or something that lives in the tree? What does your child think?

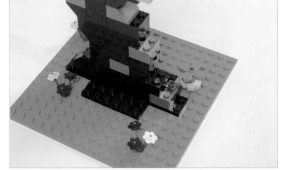

STEP 5

When you've finished adding the green leaves, finish your tree off at the top with a green plate brick and some green roof tile bricks. These tile bricks will give the top of your tree a nice rounded look.

STEP 6

Finally, add some outdoor details to the tree, such as flowers around the roots and pinecones on the greenery. Why not give your finished tree pride of place where everyone can see it?

Motor Boat

Specialty pieces needed:

• Mini antenna

One of my first experiences on a boat was a trip across the Irish Sea on a family holiday. To say it was a bumpy ride would be an understatement, but as rough as the ride was, it still offers fond memories. This LEGO build is of a motor boat perfect for carrying cargo or passengers. It's even better if you have a blue baseplate to place it on, but remember, don't try playing with it in the bath as it's not watertight!

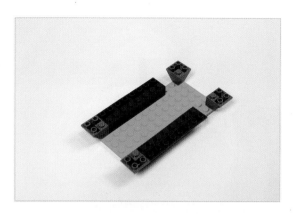

STEP 1

Find a small baseplate for the bottom of your boat. Along the sides, add inverted roof tile bricks and corner pieces on each corner of the baseplate.

STEP 2

Also add inverted roof tile bricks to the bow of the boat (the front end), building them up in layers. Use simple LEGO bricks at the stern (back end), where you'll eventually add the cab.

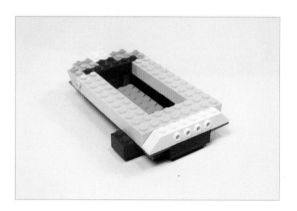

STEP 3

Start building up layers of bricks to form the hull of the boat. Keep in mind those little details that give a build character. For example, I added knob bricks to the side and back of my boat as well, so I can later add an engine grille and lights for visibility.

STEP 4

Once you're happy with how high the hull goes, use either small baseplate bricks or plate bricks to cover the hull entirely.

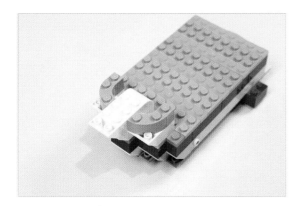

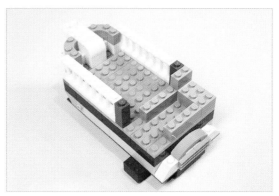

STEP 5

Continue to build up the front of your boat using "inside and out bow" bricks on either side of a centered, inverted roof tile brick. This will give the bow a nice, rounded effect.

STEP 6

Attach some fence bricks running along the side of the boat as railings to keep your passengers where they belong, then begin building the cab at the stern using some basic LEGO bricks.

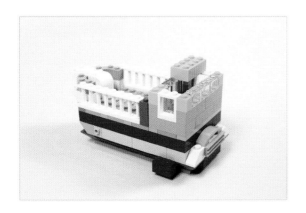

STEP 7

On the cab, be sure to add plenty of window bricks to ensure the driver of your boat can see where they're going!

STEP 8

Finish the cab off with some roof tile bricks and a plate brick on top.

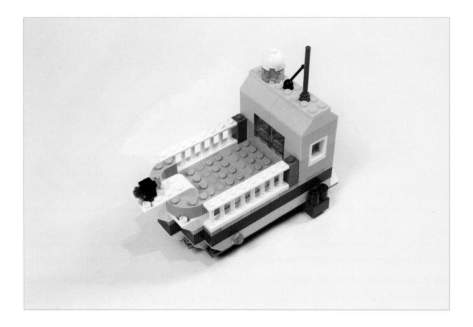

STEP 9

Finally, add all the little details you'd find on a boat in real life: antennas, a satellite dome, and plenty of lights so your boat can be seen in the dark.

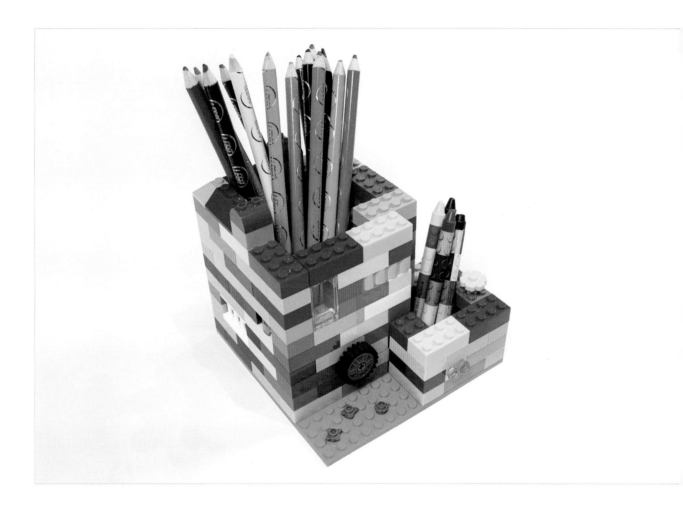

Pencil Pot

Specialty pieces needed:

- Decorative pieces (Examples: Lights, windows, flowers, wheels, etc.)

You can build lots of useful things with LEGO to help in everyday life. My son loves making things we can use and I always have a messy desk, so this build just popped into my head. A LEGO pencil pot is the perfect solution to keep things tidy. You can customize it however you like so it keeps all your different types of writing materials in one place. Plus it's quick and easy to build, in case your kids need to make a last-minute present for a family member.

STEP 1

Find a square baseplate that's big enough to hold your pencil pot. I used a 16x16 baseplate so I had room for multiple compartments.

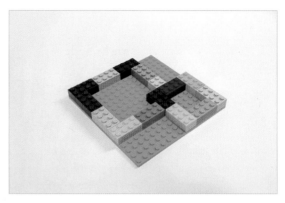

STEP 2

Lay out some basic LEGO bricks to form the shape of your pencil pot. This design will have two compartments: one big enough for pencils and pens, plus a smaller one for crayons and such.

STEP 3

Continue to build up layers with bricks. To make your pencil pot more interesting, remember to add lots of decorative pieces to its sides. From lights to windows, anything goes! If it's a gift, talk with your child about personalizing it. Does Grandpa garden? Maybe add some flowers. Enjoy biking with Mom? How about a wheel or two?

STEP 4

When you're happy your pencil pot is tall enough to store all your writing tools, put them in.

Giraffe

Specialty pieces needed:

- Two eyes

- Flower embellishment (optional)

If ever I'm struggling to find something to build with LEGO, I always turn to wildlife because my son loves trying to make the noises of different animals he sees. A giraffe is one of my favorite wildlife builds because they're big, tall, and colorful. Why not see how tall you can make yours?

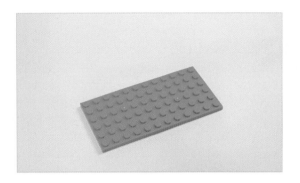

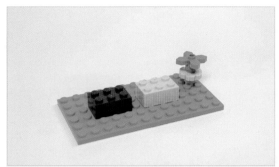

STEP 1

Find a small green baseplate that's big enough to fit your giraffe on. I wanted to make sure there was room for some foliage too, so I used a 12x6 baseplate.

STEP 2

Onto the baseplate, add a couple of bricks for your giraffe's feet. Here, I'm using two 2x3 bricks: one yellow and one brown. Try and alternate the color of the bricks to give your giraffe a stripy look.

STEP 3

Build the legs of the giraffe up using 2x2 bricks. Remember, giraffes have quite long legs so use quite a few here.

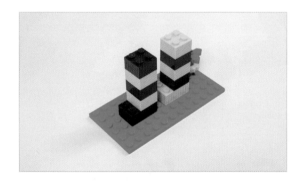

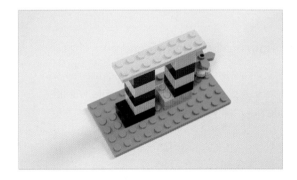

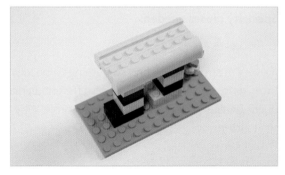

STEP 4

Use a plate brick to attach the two legs together, and then on top of this, attach some 4x1x1 bow bricks along the length of the body.

STEP 5

On top of the 4x1x1 bow bricks, build up basic yellow and brown bricks of varying sizes and shades to make the body of your giraffe.

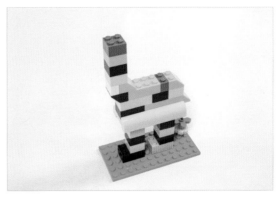

STEP 6

Once you're happy with the size of the giraffe's body, start building the neck. You may want to use some roof and inverted roof tile bricks to make the neck stick out from the body a little, then use 2x2 bricks to build up the neck. Remember, giraffes have long necks so make sure you use a good few bricks to build it up, otherwise you'll end up with a llama!

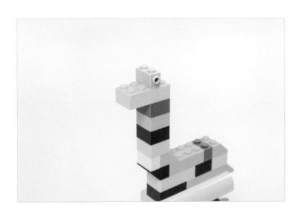

STEP 7

At the top, use a 2x4 brick to create a nose and place a couple of 1x1 knob bricks on top so you can attach some eyes later on.

STEP 8

Finally, add some roof tile bricks to round off the giraffe's nose, some 1x1 round bricks for horns, and a red 1x1 plate round for a tongue. Attach a couple of eyes to the knob bricks, and then your big friendly giraffe is complete.

Alphabet

Specialty pieces needed:

• None

Teaching the alphabet can be a tedious task at times, but a great way to make it more fun is to encourage kids to build letters using LEGO bricks. It's so much more interactive than just learning from a book, plus, you can make it a game. For example, build letters to spell your names, or build the first letter of a color's name using bricks of that color only. This way, not only are your kids learning the alphabet, they're also practicing their colors and spelling. Even better, building letters requires hardly any bricks, making it a perfect game to play when out and about.

STEP 1

Some letters, such as "A," can be made with just basic bricks. Using 2x2, 2x4, and 2x6 bricks, try creating a simple letter like this.

STEP 2

For letters that are a bit more complicated with curved edges, try using roof tile and inverted roof tile bricks to achieve that curved look, like with this "B."

STEP 3

Don't give up! You can build any letter or number using basic LEGO bricks. For challenging ones, such as "Q," you may need to spend a while longer figuring out which bricks to use and where to make the letter look right to you, but a little creativity will save the day.

Rainbow

Specialty pieces needed:

- Trees
- Flowers

Types of weather may not be the first thing that comes into your mind when thinking of what to build with LEGO, however, this rainbow build is brilliant, it's super colorful and uses LEGO baseplates so you can really set the scene. Plus, rainbows have an undeniable "Wow!" factor for kids. Whether it's a green or blue baseplate you use, you can build the perfect rainbow both on land and at sea—and you'll finally have an answer to all those questions like, "Where does the rainbow start?" and, "How big is a rainbow?"

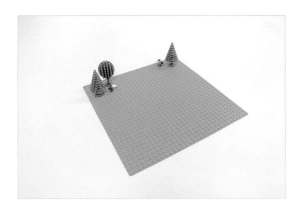

STEP 1

Find a large baseplate, then decorate it. I'm using a green one so I've added some trees and flowers to mine.

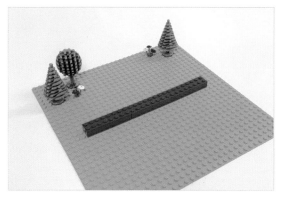

STEP 2

Next, add a line of six 2x4 dark-blue basic LEGO bricks for your rainbow to sit on. Make sure the bricks are centered in the middle of the baseplate.

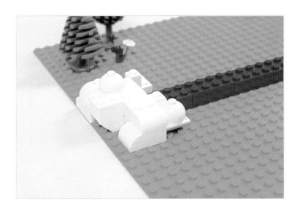

STEP 3

Now it's time to add some clouds to either side of your rainbow. To do this use basic white LEGO bricks, roof tile and inverted roof tile bricks, as well as any other quirky bricks you can find like "final" and 2x3 arch bricks too. A random assortment of white bricks will make your clouds look really cool.

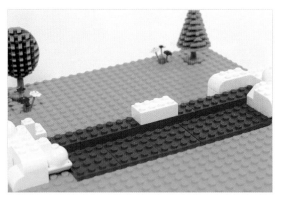

STEP 4

To simulate the space beneath a rainbow's arch, place one 2x4 white brick in the middle of the row of dark blue bricks. In the next steps you'll build the colors around it.

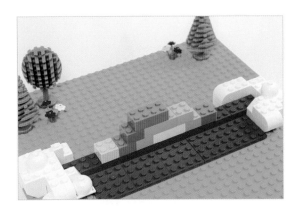

STEP 5

For the first layer of color, place a light-blue 2x2 brick at the base of the rainbow on either side of the white brick. Stack another 2x2 brick on top of each light-blue brick, but offset by one (building them up like steps) until the color reaches the top of the rainbow. Then use 2x4 bricks to run the color along the top of the rainbow, connecting the two stair-steps of color.

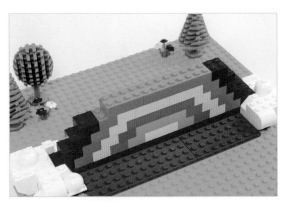

STEP 6

Repeat step 5 for each rainbow band, building your colors up until you've added five colors that fill the space between the two clouds. I built a classic rainbow—blue, green, yellow, orange, and red—but maybe your kids have other ideas.

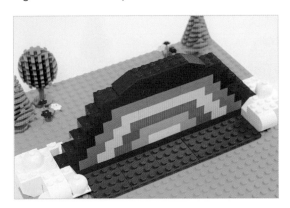

STEP 7

Finally, finish the top off with two red roof tile bricks with a 2x4 red brick in between, and then your rainbow is complete—all the beauty without the rain.

Bird

Specialty pieces needed:

- Flowers
- Eyes

Birds are another one of my favorite wildlife builds. When my family struggles for inspiration, all we do is take a look into the garden or flick through a magazine. If we see a bird we like, we build it!

Don't feel you have to stop when your bird is finished. It's also great fun to build a home for your bird too. Whether it's a cage or tree, can you create the perfect home for your bird to live in?

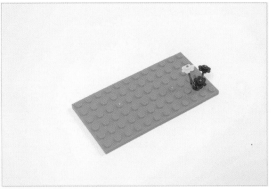

STEP 1

Find a small 12x6 green baseplate to build your bird on. Add some decoration; my bird needed flowers, for example.

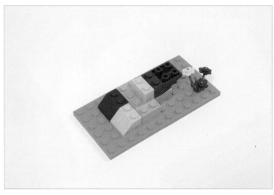

STEP 2

To build the bird's feet, use two 2x2 roof tile bricks side by side to create two claws. Behind these, add regular and inverted roof tile bricks to start building up the body and tail at the back, as shown.

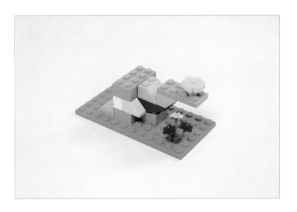

STEP 3

Keep extending the tail using more roof tile bricks and plate bricks. I also added a yellow flower brick onto the end of the tail to give it a nice finishing touch.

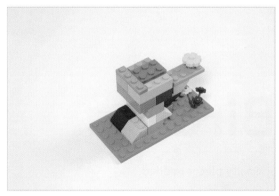

STEP 4

Continue by building up the body of your bird using regular 2x4 bricks. Then add a 1x4 and 2x3 plate brick to the top, as shown.

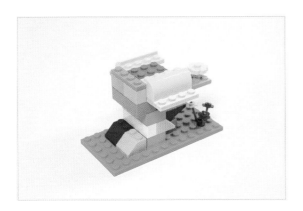

STEP 5

For the wings, I used a couple of yellow 4x1x1 bow bricks and attached these around the plate bricks on top of the body of the bird. Then add a 2x4 plate brick to the bottom of each 4x1x1 bow brick.

STEP 6

The bird needs a head: Use some basic bricks to build it up, ensuring you have a yellow or orange brick poking out at the front for the beak.

STEP 7

For the eyes, add a couple of 1x1 knob bricks on each side of the head. Onto the back of these, add a couple of 1x1x1 arch bricks. These will give the back of your bird's head a nice rounded look.

STEP 8

Finally, to finish off the bird's head, use a roof tile brick and a plate bow brick for the front. Then add an eye to each knob brick. Then your bird is complete.

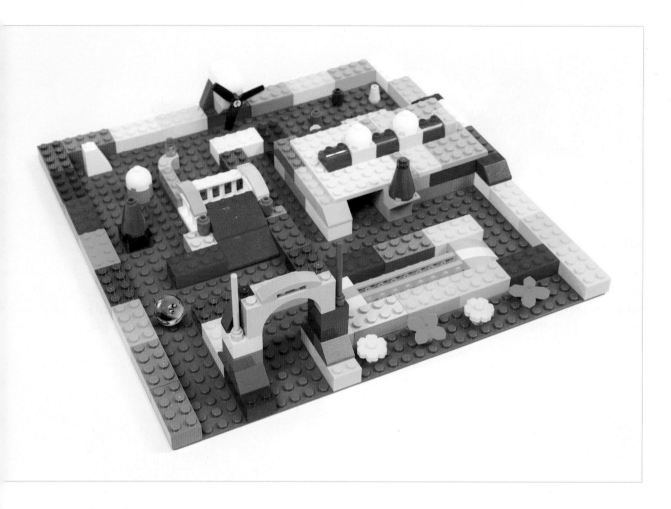

Maze

Specialty pieces needed:

- Propeller
- Marble

- Flowers and other
  embellishments as desired

LEGO is also great for building maze games. I actually built my first maze using DUPLO® bricks on a massive baseplate. As my son has grown up, we've switched to LEGO bricks.

To play the game you'll need a marble; the objective is to tilt the maze to roll the marble to the finish line. This example shows just one possibility. You can make your maze as challenging as you like by adding various routes and quirky bricks.

Why not make it a progressive game? The first one to complete the maze gets to design the next one. Or, you each build one then swap. Can your son complete Mom's maze before she can maneuver through his?

It's a great way to make LEGO even more fun to play with.

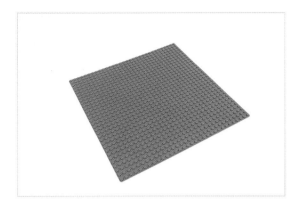

STEP 1

Begin with a baseplate. The bigger the baseplate you choose, the better, as you'll be able build a bigger, more impressive maze.

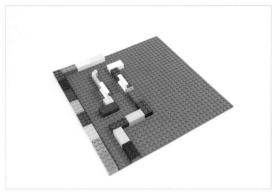

STEP 2

Next, you'll need to map out the various routes a marble can travel by adding basic LEGO bricks to the baseplate. Also line all edges of the baseplate with bricks—otherwise your marble could fall off and roll away.

STEP 3

Add multiple routes to your maze, and double-check that they're all wide enough for the marble to travel through.

STEP 4

Try building a jump using 3x4 roof tile bricks and a trap of fence bricks. It you approach the ramp too slowly, you could risk losing the marble into the cage made from fence bricks. What other traps can you devise?

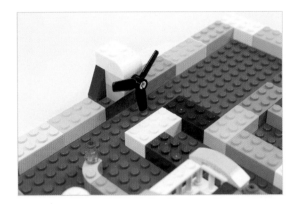

STEP 5

Another great little feature you can add to your maze is a propeller. Positioning one as shown means each time a marble passes by it'll spin the propeller.

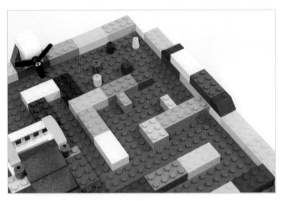

STEP 6

Be sure to add various obstacles onto your maze to make it more challenging when playing it. You can use all types of bricks to do this, including various types of 1x1 bricks.

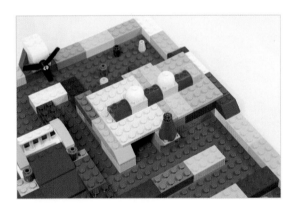

STEP 7

For an even bigger challenge, try adding a tunnel like this one to your maze. Be sure to place some obstacles underneath and build the walls high enough so your marble fits inside.

STEP 8

Why not build a track for the marble to travel along? To make a track, fix two 1x8 plate bricks onto the baseplate at a right angle. Then place some 3x1 bow bricks at either end to act like a ramp onto the track.

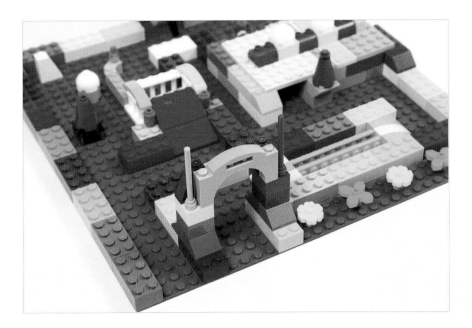

STEP 9

Finally, build a finish line at the end to signify completing the maze. Make it as spectacular as you!

Night-light

Specialty pieces needed:

- Flashlight

- Quirky bricks and embellishments to decorate

Sometimes bedtime just doesn't go smoothly, especially if your child has had a fun-packed day and they're finding it difficult to wind down. I've found building a LEGO night-light is a great way to entertain your kids in the evening and convince them to go to sleep as well. It allows them to continue playing, and then encourages them to relax with the calming light given off by a night-light they've built themselves.

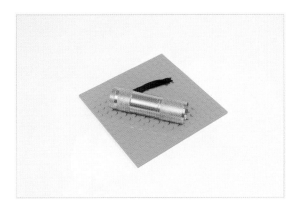

STEP 1

Find a 16x16 baseplate and a small battery powered LED flashlight of about the same scale.

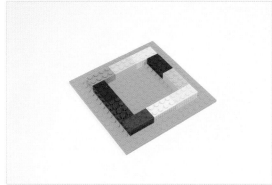

STEP 2

Next, build up a layer of 2x4 bricks to outline the base of the night-light. You can go with whatever shape you want, just ensure it's not too big that the light from your flashlight won't shine through—or so small that it won't fit.

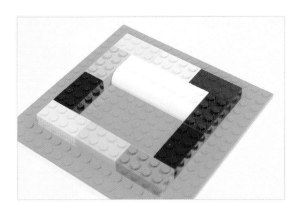

STEP 3

Add some white 2x3 arch bricks along one edge of the inside of the night-light. Adding these white bricks will reflect the light from the flashlight upwards through the night-light.

STEP 4

At the back of the night-light where the flashlight handle will sit, add bricks to keep your flashlight secure and for it to rest on when it's slotted in. A couple of basic 2x4 bricks as well as some roof tile bricks worked well for me.

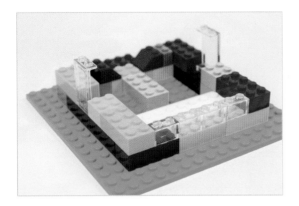

STEP 5

Now you can build the sides of your night-light up. Ensure you use plenty of see-through and window bricks for all the light to shine through. Use regular bricks between these to fill in the gaps.

STEP 6

Ensure you leave enough space at the back of the night-light so you can insert the head of the flashlight. Then add a long brick running across the top of the hole so you can continue building up your night-light.

STEP 7

Once you're happy with the height and number of see through bricks, place a suitably sized small baseplate or multiple plate bricks on top.

STEP 8

If you like, decorate the top with some quirky LEGO pieces!

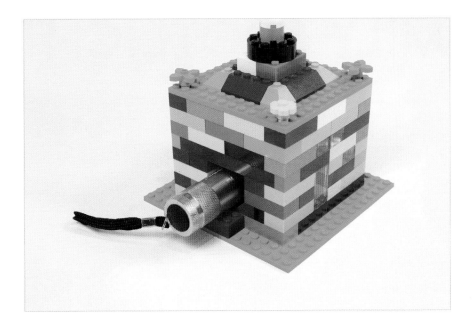

STEP 9

Finally, when you're happy with the look of your night-light, place the LED
flashlight through the hole in the back, turn it on, and enjoy the relaxing effect
of your homemade LEGO night-light.

FAMILY SPOTLIGHT

Parent: Lauren Lessard
Kids: Zack, 7 and Cole, 4
Location: Anchorage, Alaska

What do you enjoy most about building with your child?

I love building environments (ocean, jungle, desert, etc. themes—the first scene is a coral reef!) with the kids. To be honest, they are way more creative than me! They think in multiple dimensions and envision worlds that are beyond what us rigid adults could imagine.

What are your kid's favorite projects to build?

They get most excited about building scenarios that have rescuers—stretching the narrative that kids can save the world. They make up elaborate stories and play for hours, modifying the scene as they go. It's a joy to watch and listen to—particularly during our dark winter days.

Do you and/or your kids have a dream LEGO project they'd like to build?

Their dream LEGO project is an underwater marine rescue station that saves deep sea animals.

4

Fun for Everyone

Encouraging imaginative play and ways to use LEGO with everyday items, the builds in this chapter range from functional to fun, from photo frames to airplanes, and even builds that involve your smartphone. You may need a few more bricks for the constructions in this chapter, but you'll have great fun building these with your kids because they also offer loads of interaction once built. You'll also find some great architectural pieces, such as an airport control tower and a railway station, which your kids will remember building for years to come.

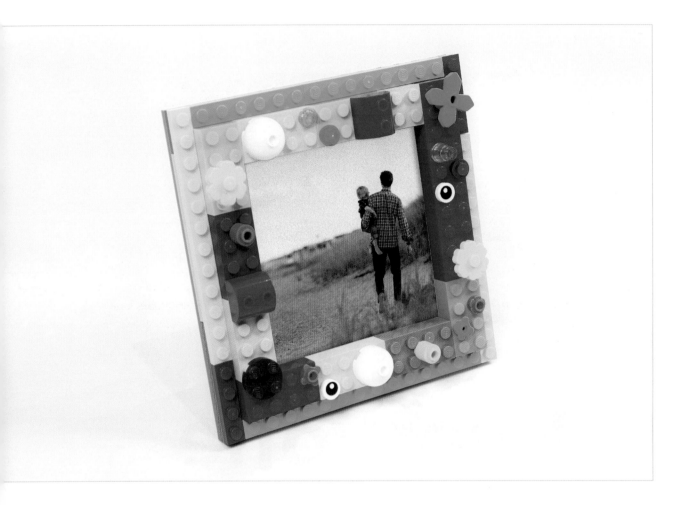

Photo Frame

Specialty pieces needed:

- Special photo or drawing
- Decorative embellishments

Thanks to smartphones we all may be taking more photos than ever, while at the same time printing fewer photos than ever. Why make the effort to print an image when we can carry it with us on our phones? Because we can put the prints of those special family moments into LEGO photo frames! What better gift than a favorite snap of a special family moment surrounded by a frame your child built? Displaying your family photos in something you've built together makes them even more special.

STEP 1

Find a baseplate that's big enough to fit your favorite photograph. Make sure your baseplate is two studs wider than your photo in both directions. Then lay plate bricks that are 2 studs wide along three of the four edges of the baseplate.

STEP 2

On the edge that has no plate bricks, lay a couple of regular bricks across from the end of one plate brick to the other, insetting the regular bricks by 1 stud. You just created the slot to slide your photograph through.

STEP 3

Attach regular bricks on top of the rest of the plate bricks along the other edges of your photo frame. Again, inset these bricks by 1 so they will extend over the frame opening and help hold your photo in place.

STEP 4

Flip your frame over, and place a couple of regular bricks on the back near what will be the bottom edge to act as a support, so the photo frame can stand up.

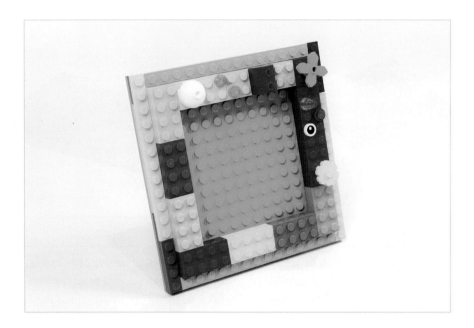

STEP 5

Now the fun part: Decorate your photo frame. Your kids can let their imaginations go wild with all kinds of decorative LEGO pieces. Use bricks that reflect the recipient's favorite color or interests for a gift, or create decorations that match the content of the photo. You could even make the frame an ever-changing art exhibit with your children's drawings inside the frame they built. Maybe when your son's drawing is inside the frame, his sister gets to add some decorations to the frame's outside. Then when it's your daughter's turn to have her drawing in the frame, he gets to add some more decorations.

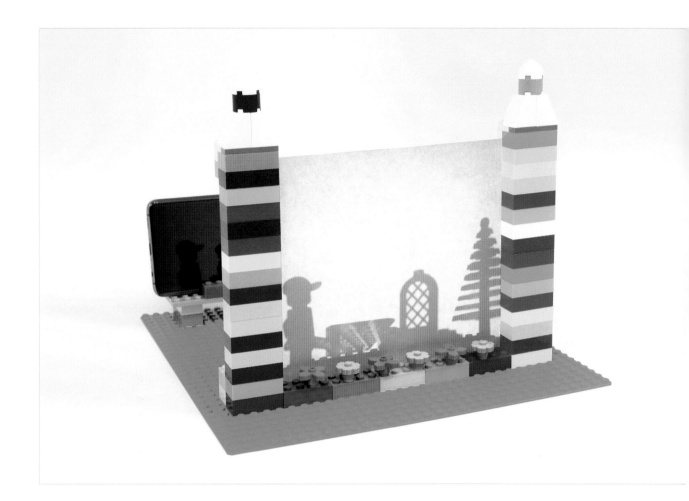

Shadow Puppet Theatre

Specialty pieces needed:

- Sheet of paper
- Smartphone
- Props for shadows

I was first inspired to build a shadow puppet theatre with my son when he used to play with DUPLO. Since then, we've perfected the same build using LEGO and a smartphone to provide the light source.

The shadow puppet theatre is fun to build and sparks kids' imaginations and story-telling abilities. It's a great excuse to think up all kinds of funny stories, and then act them out using LEGO props and people. You could even record your shadow puppet shows to send to friends and family.

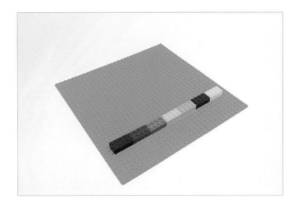

STEP 1

Find a 32x32 large baseplate, and then add a row of seven 2x4 basic LEGO bricks about an inch from the front edge (as shown). These will form the base at the front of your shadow puppet theatre.

STEP 2

Add some decorative LEGO pieces to the front brick row, then build a column on either side of it for the sides of your theatre. Each column is 16 bricks high.

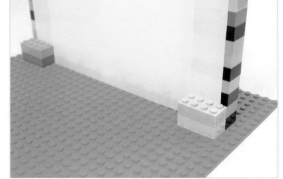

STEP 3

Rest an 8.5x5.5-inch (or A5) sheet of paper horizontally against the back of the columns. Remember, you can cut an 8.5x11-inch (or A4) sheet of paper in half to make it the correct size.

STEP 4

With the paper in place, build a couple of basic LEGO bricks up against the two columns with the paper in between so the paper doesn't move.

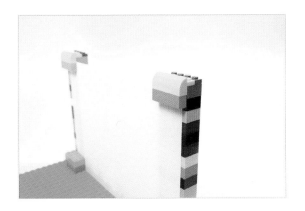

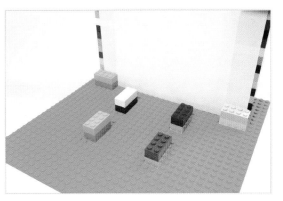

STEP 5

Attach a couple of 4x1x1 bow bricks to the top-rear of the columns to fix the paper in place at the top. Add some 4x1 plate bricks to the top-front of the columns to level them off, then decorate them if you like.

STEP 6

Start to build a stage behind the sheet of paper by attaching some basic LEGO bricks to act as supports for a platform.

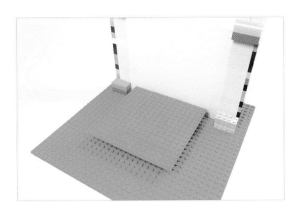

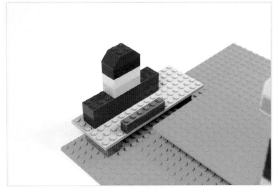

STEP 7

Add a 16x16 baseplate on top of these supports. This baseplate is the stage from where the props and actors will cast shadows onto the paper.

STEP 8

Behind the stage, build another platform designed to hold a smartphone steady on its side so it can shine its flashlight at the paper.

STEP 9

Turn the smartphone's light on, and then rest the phone in the platform. Ensure it casts light onto the sheet of paper at the correct angle so light passes past anything that stands on the stage.

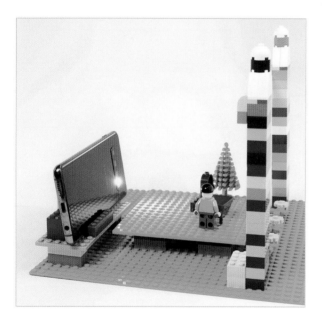

STEP 10

Now the shadow theatre is ready to put on your family's first show! Build a selection of LEGO props and use them to create a cool shadow puppet story.

House with a Pitched Roof

Specialty pieces needed:

- Bracket brick
- Additional roof tile bricks
- Additional fence bricks
- Tree
- Flowers
- Doors and windows

When I was younger and stuck for ideas for things to build, my parents generally suggested a house. Although this was fun to build the first few times, it started to get boring, so I decided that each time I built a house I would make it more special. If you're looking for inspiration and ways to make your own house unique, just look out your front window to see what features your neighbors' houses have. Or, you and the kids could go on a scavenger hunt for new house ideas by taking a walk or bike ride together. Spot an interesting chimney, roofline, or porch? Snap a photo or add it to a list of ideas.

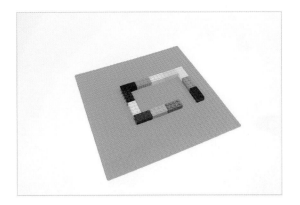

STEP 1

Start with a large green baseplate and begin lay-ing basic LEGO bricks for the base of your house. (I made mine four and a half bricks by three.) Be sure to leave room for a door and some space to the left for a carport that you'll build later.

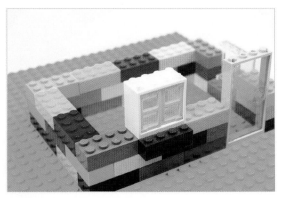

STEP 2

Continue adding additional layers of bricks to the walls of your house along with a door and window ledge for the front window.

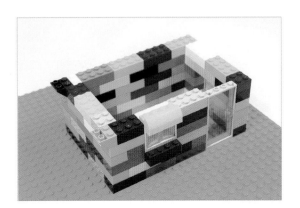

STEP 3

Once the walls of your house reach the top of the window and door, add a 4x1x1 bow brick to the top of the window. Also add two inverted roof tile bricks to the left-side corners of the house (as shown). In a few steps, you'll attach the carport to these.

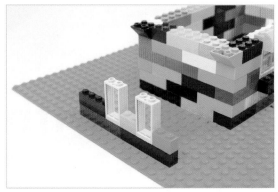

STEP 4

Begin building the sidewall of your carport, incorporating a couple of small windows too. Ensure this wall is built in a position that you can attach it to the main structure of the house with a medium (16x16) baseplate brick.

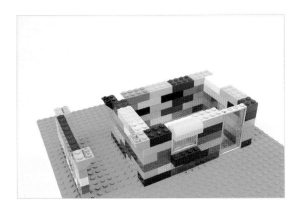

STEP 5

When the carport wall is one brick lower than the height of the house wall, add another couple of inverted tile bricks to its front and back as attach points. Level off the wall with a brick between these.

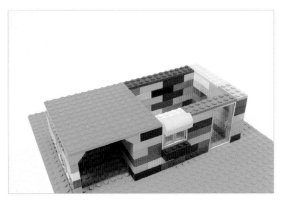

STEP 6

Use a medium-sized baseplate brick to attach the carport wall to the house. This will also act as the floor of your balcony. Also place a layer of x2 wide plate bricks around the top of the house wall to ensure it's all level with the balcony.

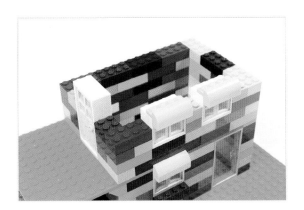

STEP 7

Continue to add bricks to make the second story, including a couple more windows (with 4x1x1 bow bricks on top) and a door leading out to the balcony. Then continue to build the second story wall up to the top of the balcony doorframe.

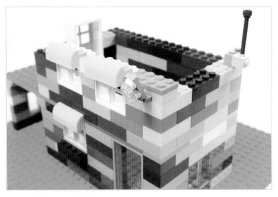

STEP 8

Why not add a couple of special details too? You can include an antenna on the side of the house using a couple of knob bricks and an antenna piece. You can also try adding an outside light like the one shown in Chapter 2. Use a LEGO bracket with some light bricks attached.

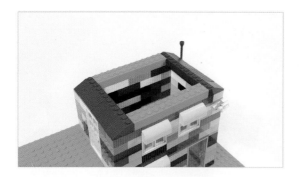

STEP 9

With the walls finished, it's time to start building the roof of the house. Simply begin layering up roof tile bricks starting from the left and right side. Also use basic bricks for a ridgeline for the front and back, to close up the gaps.

STEP 10

Once the roof tiles join in the middle, leave some space at the back of the roof to build a chimney. I also included some mini windows in the ridge-line for an attic room.

STEP 11

Use some basic LEGO bricks to build the chimney, and finish the top off with a 2x2 circle brick and a round brick on top of that.

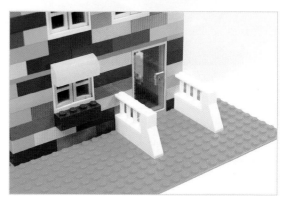

STEP 12

For finishing touches, be sure to add a railing around your balcony. I used some gate bricks, and I added embellishments on either side of the front door.

STEP 13

Finally, plant plenty of flower bricks and a tree to make your house nice and welcoming.

Car Trailer

Specialty pieces needed:

• Tow bar socket

LEGO cars are great fun, but you can make them even more exciting by building a trailer to attach to the back. You can start by building the car in Chapter 3 and adapting it with a tow bar to attach a trailer.

Depending on how high you make the sides, you can also convert this trailer into a camper. It's a great build that can be adapted in lots of different ways, depending on what you want the trailer to carry. Whether you're towing bricks, a LEGO tree, or even another car, finding ways to adapt the trailer depending on its purpose makes it brilliant for problem solving.

STEP 1

Start by building the car project in Chapter 3 (or one of your own designs), and add a tow bar brick to the back. Secure it into place using plate bricks as shown.

STEP 2

Find a small baseplate to become the base for your trailer. I chose the same size one as the one I used for my car, but if you need to haul larger gear, feel free to make yours bigger. Add a row of simple LEGO bricks along the middle of the baseplate; you'll attach the wheels to these later. Leave a gap at the end for a tow bar socket.

STEP 3

In the gap, attach a tow bar socket piece. This is what will connect the trailer to your car. Use additional plate bricks when attaching the tow bar socket to ensure the trailer is level with the car when attached. If you built the car in Chapter 3, you'll need to attach the tow bar to one plate brick on the underside of the car. Then you'll need to attach the tow bar socket piece to two plate bricks on the underside of this trailer.

 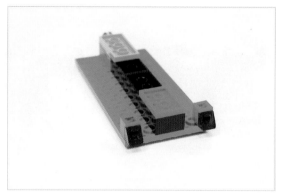

STEP 4

To the rear of the trailer add some brake lights using a couple of 1x1 knob bricks with a red light brick attached to each.

STEP 5

To attach the wheels and wheel arches, first attach some x1 wide inverted tile bricks around where the wheels will sit. Next, attach a couple of bearing element bricks onto the bricks on the trailer underside. Clip on four medium-sized rims with tires attached.

STEP 6

Flip the trailer over, then add a layer of plate bricks down the center, leaving space around them so you can attach bricks for the side of your trailer.

STEP 7

At the rear, attach two plate bricks with vertical forks on either corner of the trailer to serve as the hinge bases for a moveable ramp at the back of the trailer.

STEP 8

Add a layer of flat tile bricks onto the plate bricks you placed on the trailer in step 6, then add a layer of x1 wide bricks around the tile bricks for the trailer sides.

STEP 9

For the trailer sides, build up as many layers of bricks as you like. At this point you may even decide to build a camper instead!

STEP 10

To complete the ramp, attach a stub brick to each of the vertical fork bricks on the rear of the trailer. Attach the two stub bricks together using basic LEGO bricks and plate bricks, then push the ramp upwards to close.

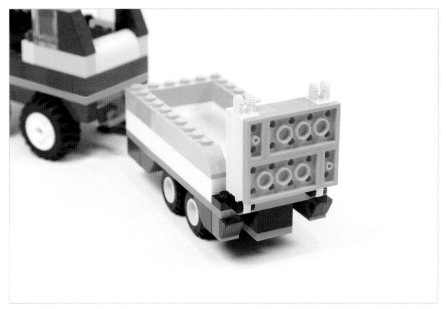

STEP 11

Finally, connect the car and trailer together, and drive off for deliveries or adventures.

Airplane

Specialty pieces needed:

- 1 left and 1 right large wing brick
- 1 left and 1 right small wing brick
- 4 1x6 reverse bow bricks
- Flat tile bricks
- Grille bricks

If your family is anything like mine, then your vacation starts the minute you arrive at the airport. The first glimpse of a plane on the runway gets the kids excited—which makes a LEGO airplane the perfect build. Not only will it get your little ones really excited about jetting off on vacation, it will also occupy their minds while waiting to take off.

One of my go-to airplanes, this project has lots of little details that makes it perfect to build with your kids. When you do arrive at the airport—or see any plane—you can make a game of trying to spot the parts you put on your LEGO airplane on a real life one, too. Don't let size limit you either! As time goes on, why not go bigger and better with a two-story jumbo jet?

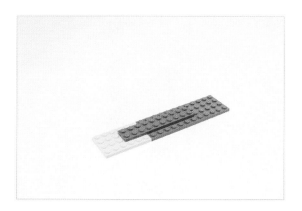 

STEP 1

Start by lining up a couple of small, x4 wide baseplates to form the base of the fuselage. Attach them together with a x2 wide plate brick. Also add a couple of plate bricks to the front to form the base of the nosecone, as shown.

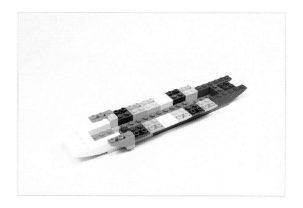 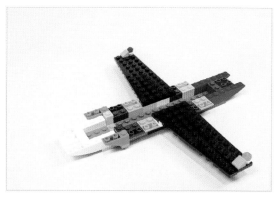

STEP 2

Lay inverted roof tile bricks facing outward along the long edges of the baseplate. Use longer, 1x6 reverse bow bricks for the nose and tail end of the airplane.

STEP 3

Add large wing bricks to either side of the fuse-lage. For even more realism, you can also add some winglets and strobe lights onto the end of each wing.

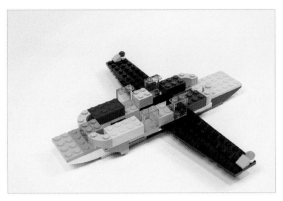

STEP 4

As the wings have made the fuselage uneven, use plate bricks to make the surface the same level so you can build up the sides of the airplane.

STEP 5

Build up the sides of the airplane using basic LEGO bricks along with window pieces and "inside and out bow" bricks for the front and back of the main cabin.

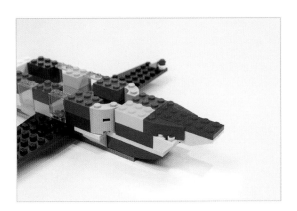

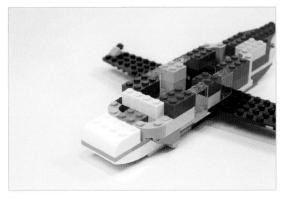

STEP 6

To start building the tail end of the aircraft, use inverted roof tile bricks, a 4x4 18° brick and plate bricks to build a surface strong enough and large enough to hold the tail, which you'll add later.

STEP 7

For the nose of the airplane, start by using a couple of arch bricks to create that curved look.

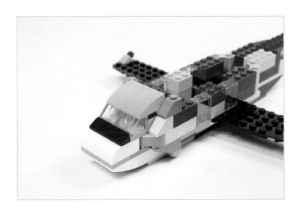

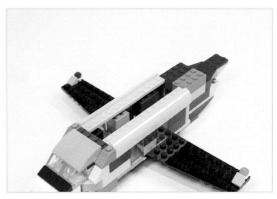

STEP 8

Then use roof tile bricks and see-through roof tile bricks for the cockpit window. Finish the front off with four 1x3 bow bricks on top of the cockpit window, then you should have a nice aerodynamic front.

STEP 9

To continue that common cylindrical look, run 4x1x1 bow bricks along the top of each side of the airplane fuselage between the nose and tail sections.

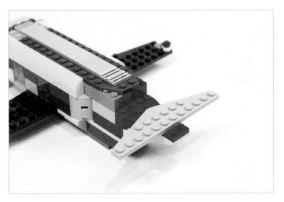

STEP 10

Now add multiple plate bricks on top with a 18° 2x4 plate brick at the tail end to streamline the roof. Also run flat tile bricks along the center of the roof, finished off with grille bricks at either end.

STEP 11

Back to the tail of the aircraft: This time, add a couple of small wing bricks across the rear of the tail section you built earlier.

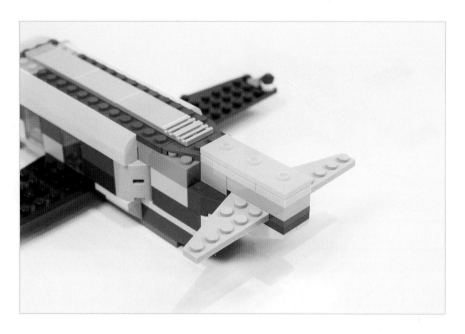

STEP 12

On top of the small wing bricks, place on some regular and plate bricks then add a row of three 2x2 1 knob plate bricks. You want these to sit one row higher than the top of the plane. In a few steps you'll place the tail on these bricks, and they'll allow the tail to sit centrally on the airplane.

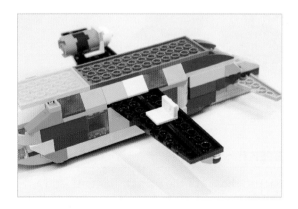
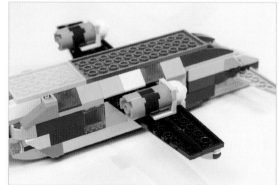

STEP 13

Flip the aircraft upside down so you can add the jet engines. These are really simple to build. Start by placing an angle plate brick onto the underside of each wing, then attach a row of 2x2 circle bricks onto each angle plate to make a cylinder. Then attach a "final" brick to the end of the jet engine to finish them off.

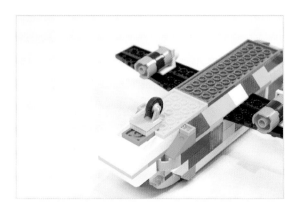 

STEP 14

Attach the front landing gear by placing a single wheel centered under the cockpit. For the rear landing gear, put a plate brick across the plane body behind the wings, centering it so two stubs extend beyond the body on either side. Add a single wheel on each side.

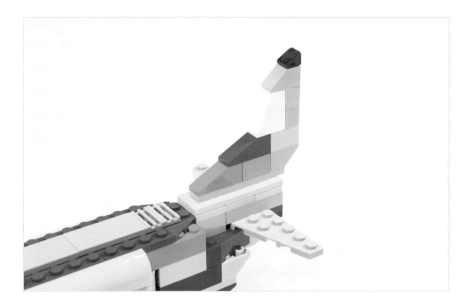

STEP 15

Build the tail simply by attaching a 1x6 plate brick to the row of 2x2 1-knob plate bricks at the rear of the plane. To this, attach longer tile bricks at the front for the first couple of rows of the tail, with an inverted tile brick at the back. Then use narrower tile bricks along with regular x1 wide bricks for the remaining rows. Attach a strobe to the top of the tail then your airplane is ready for take off!

Bookends

Specialty pieces needed:

- Propeller
- Eyeball
- Other embellishments as needed

If you find keeping all your family's books organized a problem, then you need some LEGO bookends! I've found building them with my son has been a great way to encourage him to read more, as he gets to use the bookends at the same time. We also update ours throughout the year. Why not consider building some themed ones during the holiday season or to give as gifts? Kids get great satisfaction from making something useful, then seeing it in use by their families.

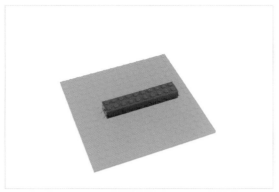

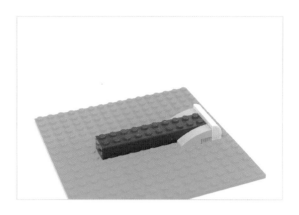

STEP 1

For each bookend, start with a square baseplate. Add a 2x10 brick running along the center of the baseplate, leaving a little extra room on one side for books to sit on.

STEP 2

Place a couple of bricks onto the end of this brick which will help support the weight of the books when stacked up against the bookends. These can be any type of brick, and here I've used 1x3 bow bricks and a 1x4x1⅓ brick.

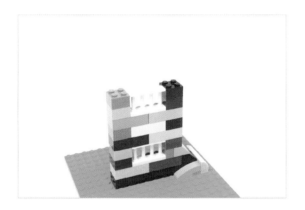

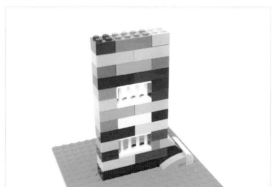

STEP 3

Now start building up your bookends. Your bookends can be any shape you like; you'll just need to make sure they're wide enough and strong enough to support the weight of your books. Here I'm building a windmill for one of my bookends.

STEP 4

You can easily turn a tower into a windmill: Once the bookend is high enough, add a snap and cross brick, then attach a four-blade propeller onto it to hold the sails.

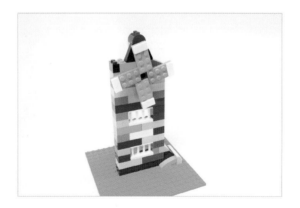

STEP 5

Attach some large sails onto the windmill brick using 2x4 plate bricks with some tiles on the end for decoration. I also added a couple of roof tile bricks to the top, to finish it off.

STEP 6

Now, build your second bookend. Remember, it doesn't have to be the same as the first; it can be whatever you like! I built an animal for the second one. Whatever you build, again make sure it's strong enough and large enough to support your books.

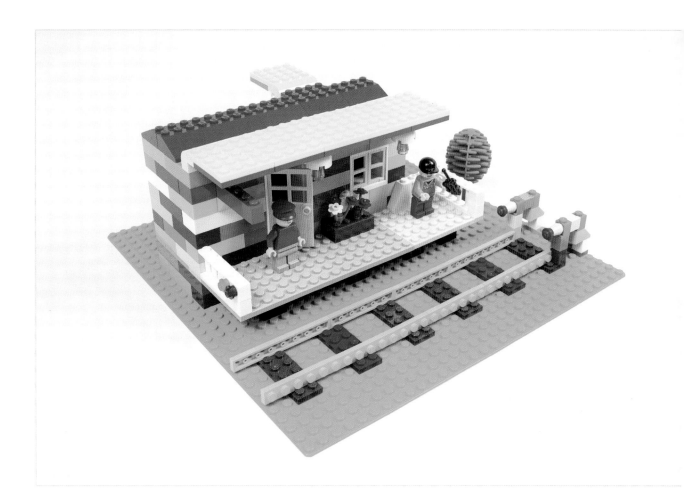

Railway Station

Specialty pieces needed:

- Additional roof tile bricks
- Tree
- Flowers
- Minifigures
- Doors and windows

My son *loves* anything with wheels, and he always loves a trip to the station where he can see all the trains. This build brings the railway station home and includes loads of little details to make it extra special.

This build really is one to be proud of and it's great fun to make as a family project. Don't worry if you don't have official LEGO track, we'll use the technique of building track with plate bricks shown in Chapter 2.

STEP 1

Find a large baseplate, and begin laying down 2x6 plate bricks as railroad ties.

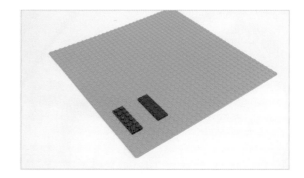

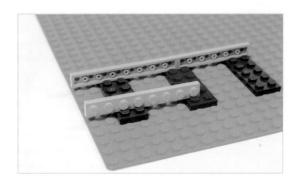

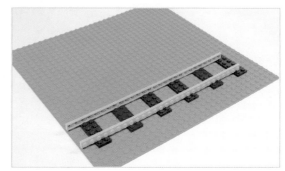

STEP 2

Next, attach some x1 wide plate bricks to the ties. Do this by snapping them into place between the studs on the tie bricks as shown.

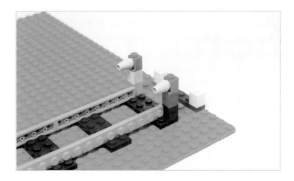

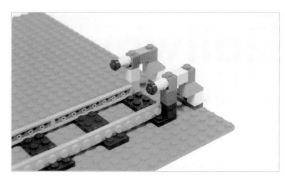

STEP 3

Leave some space at the end of the track to build a set of bumpers. These are used to prevent trains running off the end of the track. Begin building the bumpers using 1x1 bricks and attaching some nose cone bricks to some 1x1 knob bricks.

STEP 4

Then add some 1x1 round pieces to the end of the nose cone bricks and ensure the bumpers are well supported so they can absorb any impact from an oncoming train.

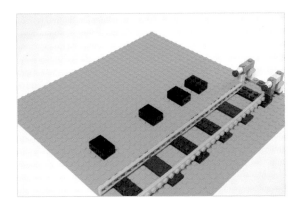 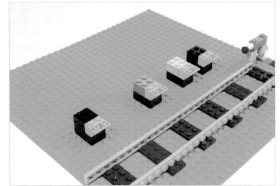

STEP 5

Now we need to begin building the platform. Start by adding the supports to raise the platform up. Use some basic bricks for the base of the supports, then add a 2x2 brick and an inverted roof tile brick on top of each.

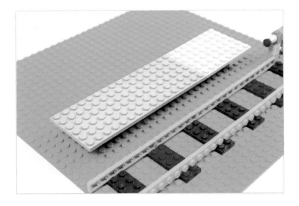 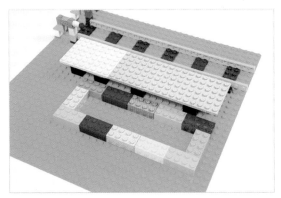

STEP 6

To build the platform, place medium-sized plate bricks on top of the supports. Make sure you use enough to run along the length of the track you have laid.

STEP 7

We now need to begin constructing the station building. Use basic LEGO bricks to start building the walls of the building. Ensure it's constructed all the way up to the edge of the platform.

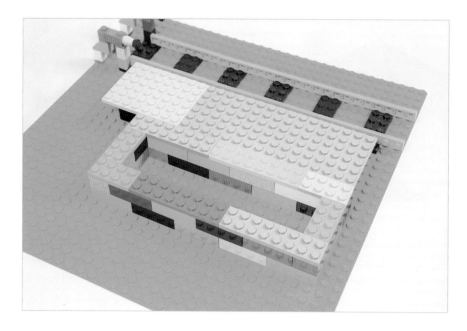

STEP 8

When the wall almost reaches the height of the platform, add a layer of plate bricks to the walls to make them level with the platform. Add another row of bricks, but be sure to leave openings for a front and rear entrance.

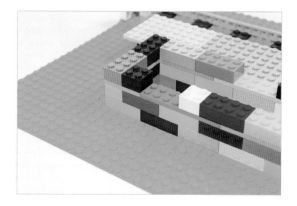 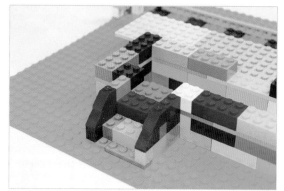

STEP 9

Because the station is raised, it needs some steps leading up to the station entrance at the rear. Build these using some simple LEGO bricks and x1 wide roof tile bricks for the staircase handrails.

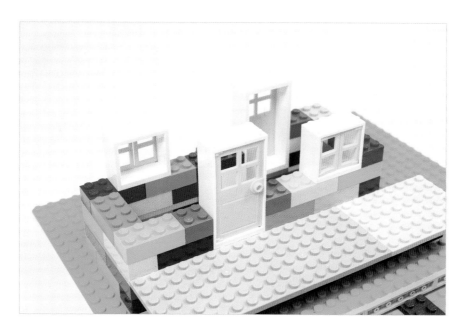

STEP 10

With the steps in place, add a door to the back and front of the station building, along with some windows. Then continue building the station building walls.

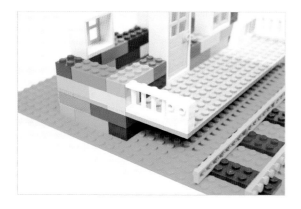 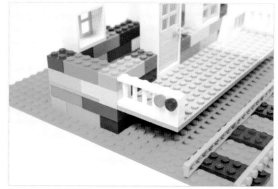

STEP 11

Also add some fencing bricks from the walls of the station building along the edges of the platform. For one of the fences, why not incorporate a start/stop signal using a double knob brick with a green and red light attached?

STEP 12

At the top of the station building, add a time-table board that pokes out above the platform. Attach a 1x6 brick to the side of the station wall, with an inverted tile brick underneath to support it.

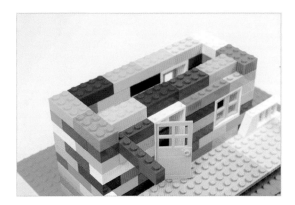

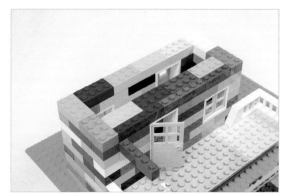

STEP 13

For the final layer of bricks at the top of the station building, on the side attached to the platform, ensure the final layer of bricks is x3 studs deep. You can achieve this by adding one row of x1 wide bricks.

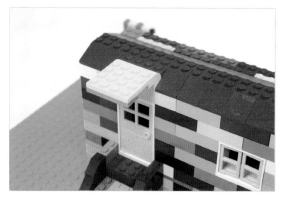

STEP 14

Place roof tile bricks on top of the station building, leaving a gap above the rear entrance door so you can attach a canopy.

STEP 15

Use a 4x1x1 bow brick and small baseplate brick above the rear door to create the canopy.

STEP 16

For the platform side, attach a row of 4x1x1 bow bricks along the length of the station building. Attach plate bricks to these bricks to create a shelter over the station platform.

STEP 17

Now it's time to add some of the finer details! You can add lighting under the platform shelter using "final" bricks with orange nose cone bricks attached. And why not add a planter to the platform by attaching some flower bricks to a brown brick?

Tractor

Specialty pieces needed:

- Chair
- Steering wheel
- Windshield
- Cyclinder brick
- Palisade bricks

"Tractor" is one of the first words my son said—it was one of the first things we built together with LEGO! Because this build doesn't require too many bricks, we've found it's a great one to build if you're travelling and have brought along only a limited amount of bricks. If you have plenty of bricks and room, you could add farm buildings and animals to go with your tractor.

STEP 1

Find a 4x6 plate brick and attach a 2x6 plate brick to the front of it (using a plate brick underneath to attach them together). You'll build the tractor cab on the 4x6 plate and the engine section on the 2x6 plate brick.

STEP 2

Attach the radiator grille to the front of the tractor by first attaching a double knob brick then a radiator grille brick.

STEP 3

For the base of the tractor, use basic bricks and "inside and out bow" bricks to build the first layer. Then add base and plate bricks on top, as shown.

STEP 4

We now need to build the wheel arches that will sit over the top of the rear wheels. To do this, attach 1x1x1 arch bricks to 2x4 plate bricks, then attach these to the side of the tractor cab. Ensure all the plate bricks here sit flush on the cab.

STEP 5

Place another layer of basic bricks on the cab and use some palisade bricks on the front section to give an engine effect. Also add a roof tile brick to the front of the engine section.

STEP 6

Join the engine and cab sections together using 1x1x1 arch bricks then place a LEGO chair and steering wheel into the cab.

STEP 7

Place some tall roof tile bricks at the back of the cab that will support the roof. I also used a couple of knob bricks, which I'll attach some brake lights to later.

STEP 8

Now use window bricks on the side of the cab and a windshield brick at the front. Also use a 4x4 plate brick for the roof.

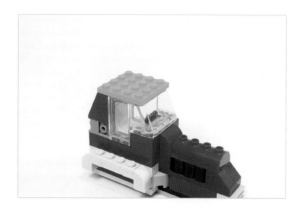

STEP 9

It's now time to add wheels. Flip your tractor upside down and attach a 2x4 wheel suspension brick at the back and two 1x2 snap and cross bricks at the front (as shown). Onto these, clip on some large wheel rims with chunky tires attached.

STEP 10

Add your finishing touches. I used a cylinder round 2x2 brick to make a strobe light on the cab roof, as well as added brake lights and a tow bar.

Airport Control Tower

Specialty pieces needed:

- Mini antenna
- Minifigure radio
- Chair
- Windows and doors
- Minifigure
- Windows

The control tower is generally always the first thing you see on the approach to an airport. If a trip to the airport is part of an upcoming vacation, you can really build the hype for your kids if you suggest constructing an airport control tower.

The sky's the limit too! Make this build as tall as you like using all your LEGO bricks. Build the airplane project alongside it, and you've got yourself a fully operational airport!

STEP 1

Find a 16x16 baseplate to build the control tower on, and then begin building the walls of your control tower. I built a larger section for the entrance and a smaller section for the tower.

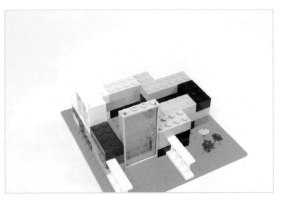

STEP 2

Build the walls of the control tower up, adding doors and windows along with fences and plants in front of it on the baseplate.

STEP 3

When you have built the walls to the height of the door, place a longer brick across the top of the tower section for extra support.

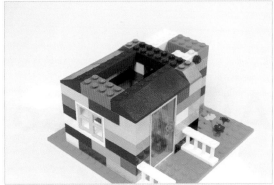

STEP 4

Finish off the entrance section by using tile bricks to provide a roof. Also insert a brick between the front and rear tiles for the ridgeline.

STEP 5

Once the roof is in place, continue building up the tower section until it's as tall as you like. I also added some lights to the side of the tower using knob bricks going up the tower.

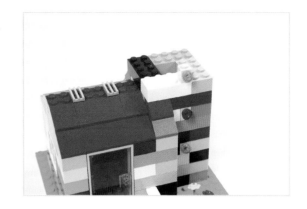

STEP 6

To prepare the top of the tower for the control center, add roof tile and plate bricks to provide a base.

STEP 7

Add a layer of inverted roof tiles around your plate bricks to make the control center bigger. Onto this, add some more plate bricks to make it easy to build on.

STEP 8

For the control center, use x1 wide bricks and "inside and out bow" bricks to build the walls. Then use window bricks and transparent bricks for the windows too. Remember to also use bricks between the windows, on the corners as well.

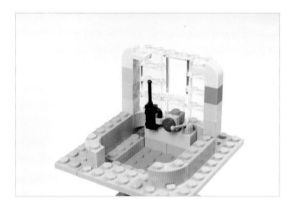
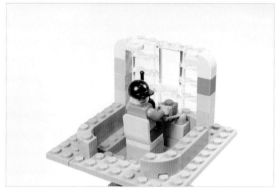

STEP 9

On the inside of the control center, build a console table using a mini antenna and utensil brick, or whatever bricks you can find that are suitable. Also add a chair for your air traffic controller to sit in.

STEP 10

Place some plate bricks on top of the windows as a roof, and also add some antenna and light bricks to the roof as well.

STEP 11

Add any more finishing touches you like, then your air traffic control tower is complete.

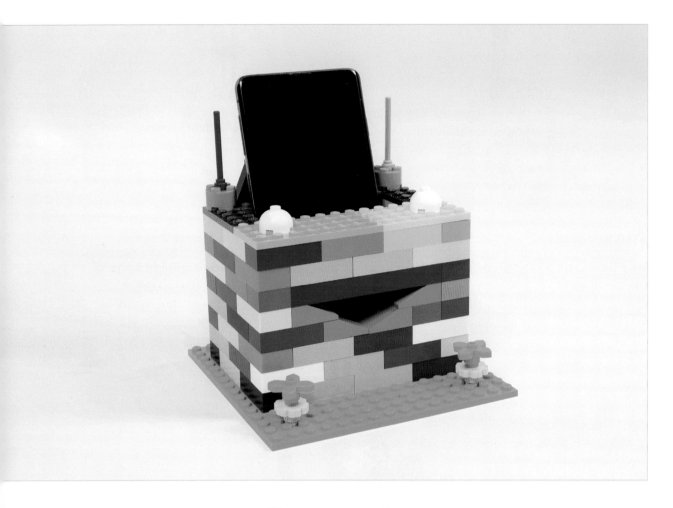

Phone Speaker

Specialty pieces needed:

- Smartphone
- Other decorative embelishments

Placing your phone in a glass can boost the bass and volume of the music playing from it. As phones have got bigger, finding a glass big enough to act as a speaker has become a struggle. We've found building a phone speaker from LEGO works just as well and you can make it big enough to fit all kinds of phones.

My family uses a LEGO phone speaker in all kinds of ways, whether it's in the garden for entertainment or the bedroom for playing lullabies when trying to get the little one to sleep.

STEP 1

Find a small baseplate and ensure your phone is at least two-thirds of the width of the baseplate.

STEP 2

Start building the speaker using basic bricks. Your phone is going to stand within the speaker, so ensure it's slightly wider than the phone you'll be using to play music.

STEP 3

We need to construct an area at the front of the speaker for sound to travel through. To do this, use roof tile bricks pointing towards each other in the middle of the speaker, as shown.

STEP 4

Use a long brick above the roof tile bricks, and then continue to build up the height of the speaker.

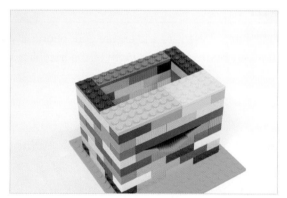

STEP 5

Ensure the speaker is tall enough so approximately one-third of your phone pokes out of the top, then add some plate bricks to the front of the speaker so the phone can slot in neatly.

STEP 6

Add some decorative bricks to your phone speaker, then slot your phone in and play some of your favorite music!

CHAPTER

5

For the Adventurous

From a train engine to a moving bridge to a gas station and even a crane, the builds in this chapter are some of my all-time favorites. Some are grand in stature and many have moving parts, but all offer loads of problem-solving opportunities to encourage your kids to use their imaginations and figure out how things work. With pulleys and gears, several of the builds in this chapter will also introduce your kids to some basic LEGO Technic bricks, including gear wheels, axles, and wedge belt wheels.

Be prepared, though: These builds may take a bit longer to construct, but that makes them great to build on a rainy day. With so many exciting elements, these builds will keep your family occupied for hours on end. I hope you enjoy building everything in this chapter as much as my family and I have.

Train Engine

Specialty pieces needed:

- 4x4 Round brick
- Clamp brick

I was really into trains when I was a kid and spent much of my childhood constructing a great train layout with my dad. Naturally, I really wanted a LEGO train set as well, so I built my own. Now, I build the engine in this chapter for my train-loving son.

As you may guess from this LEGO train engine's design, I was also a fan of a certain little blue train engine on TV. You can extend this build by attaching additional train cars. What's more, if you remove the tires from the wheel rims, you can use this engine with the train station build in Chapter 4.

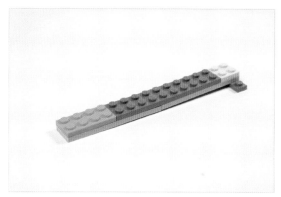

STEP 1

Choose a couple of long x2 wide plate bricks for the base of your train engine. Then attach another layer of plate bricks on top to strengthen it. These will make up the total length of your train engine, so use large ones for an extra long train or smaller bricks for a tank engine.

STEP 2

Place a square plate brick at the front of the train. This is where the train's light and buffers will sit, right at the front of the train's boiler. Also place some regular LEGO bricks along the length of the train to hold the boiler base.

STEP 3

To build the arch that will surround the top of the train wheels, place some 1x1x1 arch bricks at either end of the steam train base and connect them with long x1 wide plate bricks.

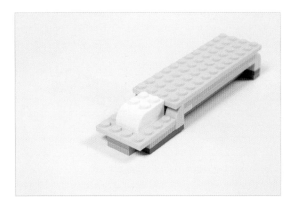

STEP 4

Place a long plate brick (that's the same width as the square one you added to the front) on top of the wheel arches. Then add a 2x3 arch brick to the front of the train.

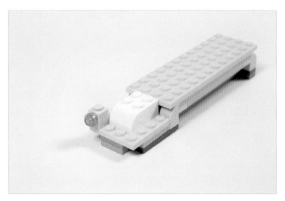

STEP 5

So your train can travel in the dark, add a light to the front section. Simply place a 1x1 knob brick to the left of the 2x3 arch brick and attach a light brick to it.

STEP 6

Now we'll start building the train's boiler. Build its bottom by lining up inverted roof tile bricks to give it that curved look. Make sure you don't line them along the entire length of the train, however, as you'll need to leave some space for the cab at the back.

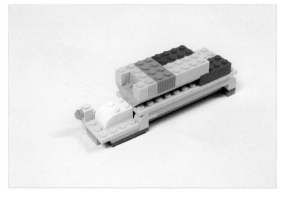

STEP 7

Use regular LEGO bricks to build up the sides of the boiler, plus add some at the back of the train to start the base of the cab. You'll be attaching a round brick to a 1x2 snap and cross brick to create the circular front of the boiler next, so be sure to leave a 1x2 space at the front of the boiler.

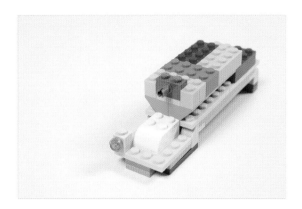 

STEP 8

Attach the snap and cross brick (on top of a 1x2 plate brick) to the front, then clip in a 4x4 round brick.

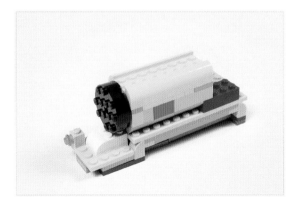 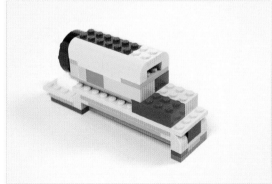

STEP 9

Line the top of the boiler with 4x1x1 bow bricks to give that circular look on top. Then attach these bricks to each other using a row of x2 wide plate bricks.

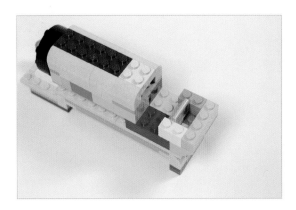
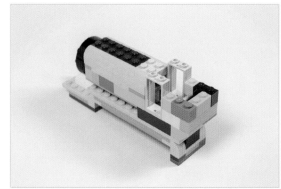

STEP 10

The cab at the back of the train needs to be separated into two areas: one to store the coal and one for your engineer to stand in. If you have one, use a clamp brick to separate the two spaces, otherwise use a 1x2 brick. Then build up the coal area with x1 wide bricks and add window bricks so your engineer can get in and out of the cab.

STEP 11

Place a 4x4 plate brick on top of the cab for a roof. Ensure there's a slight overhang at the back in order to keep the engineer and coal dry.

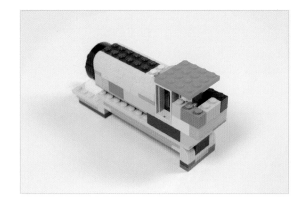

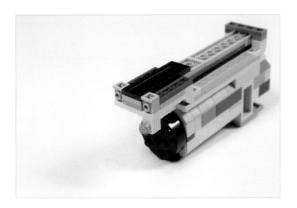
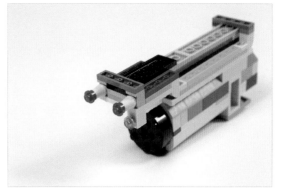

STEP 12

To help when shunting and to protect your train against collisions, it needs some buffers. Do this by attaching a couple of 1x1 knob bricks to the front of the underside of the train. Then add on a small nose cone brick with a 1x1 round brick on the end.

STEP 13

Attach all the wheels to the underside of your train. You'll need two sets of smaller wheels attached to 1x4 bearing plate bricks at the front (just behind where the buffers sit). Then you'll need three sets of larger wheels attached to 2x2 bearing element bricks at the back. To ensure they all sit level on the ground, use plate bricks underneath the smaller wheels.

STEP 14

For the finishing touches, add a smokestack to the front of the train using a 2x2 round brick with a 1x1 round brick on top. Also add a "final" brick halfway down the length of the boiler, for the steam dome. It's time to build some steam and get rolling!

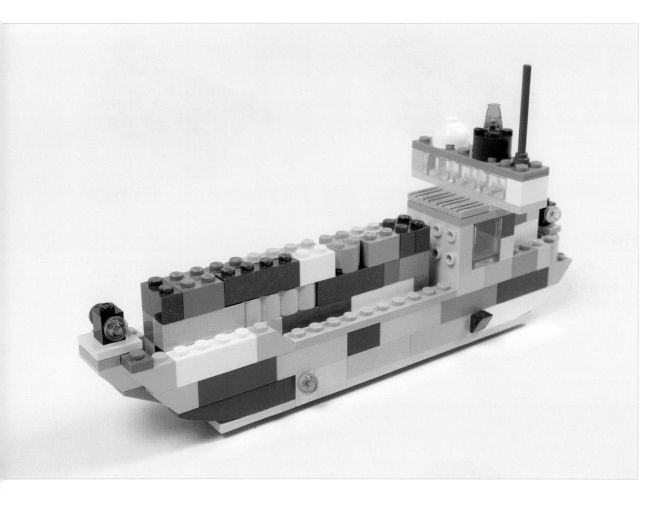

Cargo Ship

Specialty pieces needed:

- 4 1x6 reverse bow bricks
- Grille bricks
- Transparent bricks

Loaded up with cargo ready for its first sail, this LEGO cargo ship has loads of cool little details to help make it super realistic. You can make this as a miniature or as large as you like. Simply use the general principles in the steps provided and let your bricks be your guide.

You can easily put together a fully working dock alongside your cargo ship by building the crane featured later in this chapter.

STEP 1

Line up plate bricks to the length you'd like your cargo ship to be, and then attach all of these together using x2 wide plate bricks to form the base.

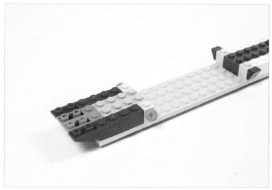

STEP 2

To form the rear section of the hull, attach inverted roof tile bricks and 1x6 reverse bow bricks, along with basic bricks to one end of the base. Also add a couple of 1x1 knob bricks (with light bricks on) on this section.

STEP 3

Repeat step 2 at the other end of the ship to form the forward section of the hull, varying the lights from the stern.

STEP 4

Build up the sides of the cargo ship's hull with regular bricks until the hull is as high as you need it to be. Continue adding inverted roof tile bricks to the front and back with each layer of bricks added, using 25° inverted roof tile bricks at the front (if you have them), to make the front more slanted.

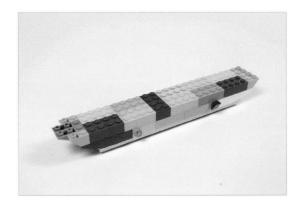

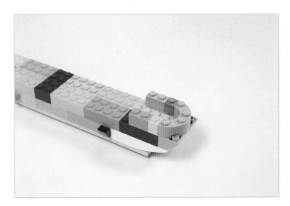

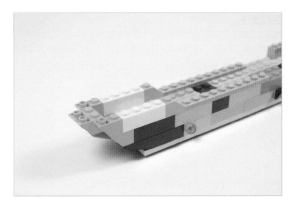

STEP 5

We now need to build the walls on the cargo ship to ensure shipping containers don't fall overboard! At the rear, use x1 wide bricks and "inside and out bow" bricks, and place roof tile bricks and x1 wide bricks at the front. For the midsection, use x1 wide plate bricks on either side of the ship.

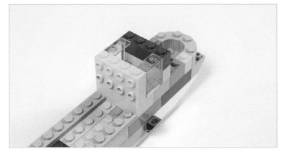

STEP 6

Next, we'll build the bridge and accommodation section of the cargo ship between the stern and midsection of the ship. Start with a layer of regular bricks, then add a couple of layers of x4 wide knob bricks and window bricks. The knob bricks give the effect of lots of porthole windows in the accommodation section.

STEP 7

Attach a plate brick for the roof and some radiator grille bricks for effect if you have them.

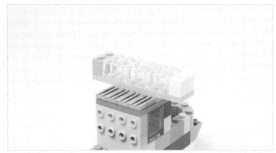

STEP 8

The bridge section of a cargo ship often overhangs either side of the hull. So, behind the grille bricks on the top of the accommodation section, attach a narrow plate brick that's longer than the width of the hull. Then attach a row of transparent bricks on top so the captain has a good view.

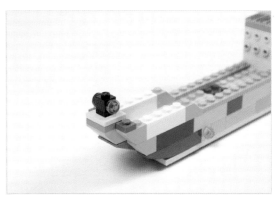

STEP 9

Add on another plate brick for the roof, and then attach bricks for an antenna, beacon, and radar.

STEP 10

Now create a bow light for the front of the ship: Attach a double knob brick with a red light brick on one side and a green light brick on the other side.

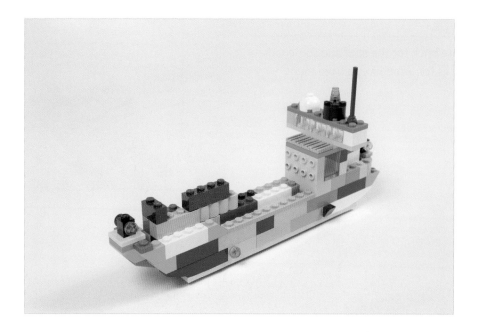

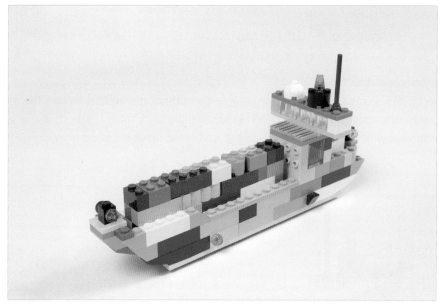

STEP 11

Your cargo ship is now ready to be loaded. Add bricks in a variety of shapes and sizes along the top of the ship's hull. Time to sail.

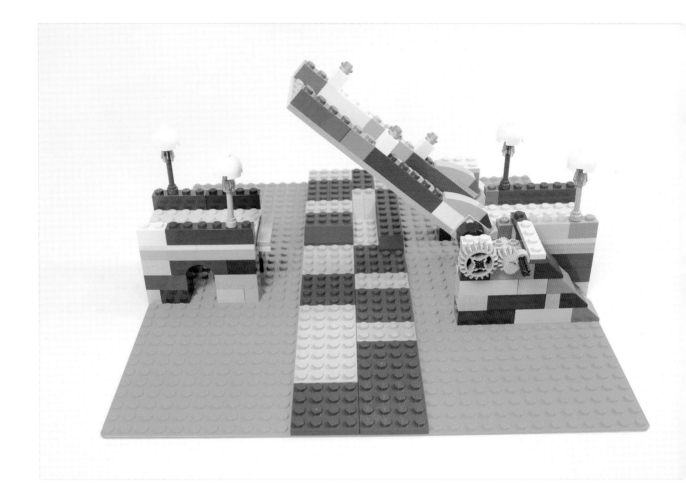

Bridge

Specialty pieces needed:

- 1x4 brick with 3 holes in
- 1x2 brick with 1 hole in
- 3 short axles
- 2½ bushes for axles
- Small gear
- Medium gear
- Axle handle

I was first inspired to build a LEGO bridge after seeing London's famous Tower Bridge. Although not as grand in stature, this build uses the same principles to draw the bridge open as Tower Bridge. A simple set of gears lifts the midsection of the bridge, making the build a great way to introduce gears and basic mechanics to your kids. My son really enjoys the challenge of understanding how the moving parts need to work for the bridge to function.

Why not try building the boat (Chapter 3) or the cargo ship in this chapter, and then challenging your kids to build a bridge big enough for the boats to fit under?

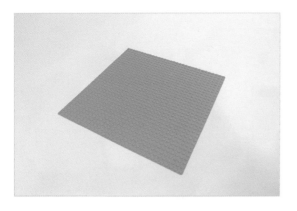
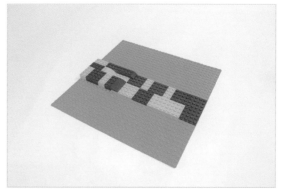

STEP 1

Find a large green baseplate, and then use plenty of blue plates and regular bricks to build a river across the center for the bridge to span.

STEP 2

Next we'll build the midsection of the bridge (the part that will lift up). Find a small baseplate brick that's long enough to pass over the river but still leaves some space either side of the river for the fixed parts of the bridge.

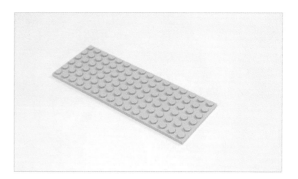

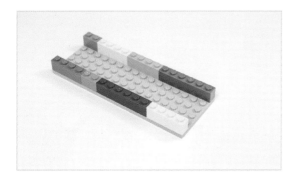

STEP 3

Attach a row of x1 wide bricks on each long side of the baseplate to act as barriers. From the top of each of the barriers at one end, attach a 2x2 angle plate brick. These bricks will fix this end of the bridge into place. Add some decorative bricks on top to further secure the angle plate bricks into place.

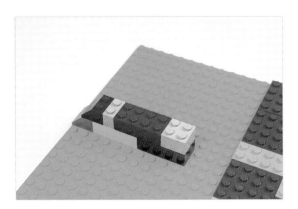
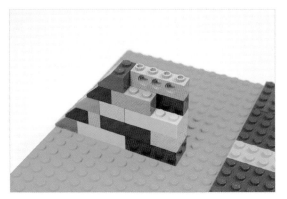

STEP 4

To create the fixed support and hinge that the bridge midsection will attach to, build a small wall and top it with a 1x4 brick with three holes. This brick should be at the height you want your bridge midsection to sit.

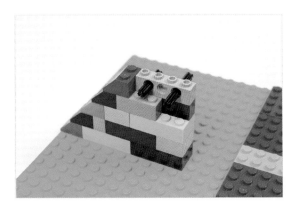
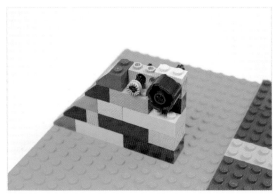

STEP 5

Insert a short axle through either end of the top brick's holes. On the axle closest to the river, attach a 2x2 round brick, and then attach a ½ bush on the other axle, as shown.

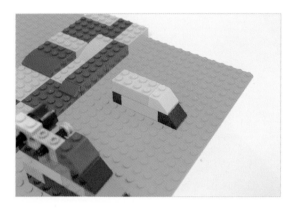 

STEP 6

On the same side of the river, build a second wall of the same size. The distance between the walls should be the same as the width of the bridge midsection. On the top of the second wall, attach a 1x2 brick with 1 hole in. Make sure this hole lines up with those on the first wall, and then attach another short axle with a ½ bush on the outside.

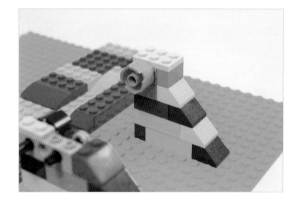 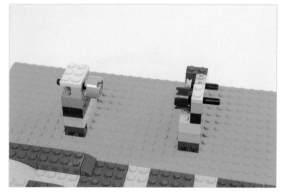

STEP 7

Attach a 2x2 round brick to the axle on the inside of the second wall. You should have two walls opposite each other for the bridge midsection to fit between.

STEP 8

With everything in place, attach the angle brick on either side of the bridge midsection to the 2x2 round brick on each wall. You may need to make some minor adjustments, such as moving the walls slightly or adjusting where the round bricks sit on the axles. Once fitted, the bridge midsection should lift freely.

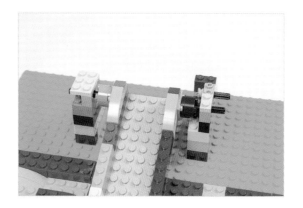

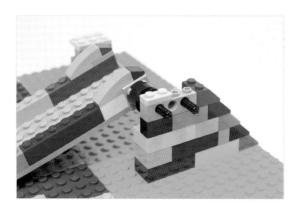

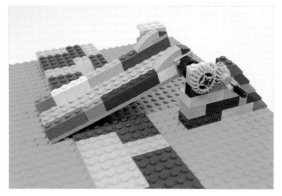

STEP 9

We're now going to attach the mechanism you'll turn to lift the bridge. On the wall that has two axles, simply place a medium gear on the axle that has the round brick attached. Place a small gear on the other axle, and ensure they make contact with each other. Having these two gears of different sizes provides a simple gear to make the bridge easier to lift. Attach a handle to the axle with the smaller cog to make it easier to turn.

STEP 10

Next, start building the road that will lead off this side of the bridge. Build up basic bricks between the two walls that support the bridge midsection.

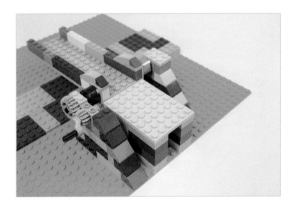
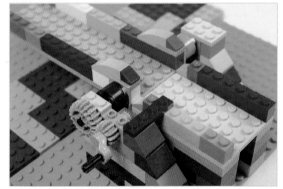

STEP 11

The road section needs to be the same height as the bridge midsection when it is level (closed position). Place a large plate brick on top of the road to even it off. Double-check it sits level with the rest of the bridge, and then add barriers to this section too, using 1x wide bricks. You can use a plate brick to secure this section into place with the wall that has the gears. Test the bridge to check that the barriers on each section don't get in the way of each other when the bridge is drawn open.

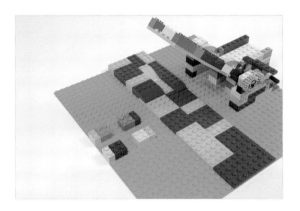

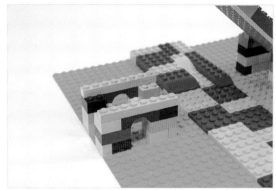

STEP 12

One good road deserves another, so build the road that leads off the other end of the bridge across the river. Again, use regular bricks and a large plate brick to build it up to a height that is the same level as the rest of the bridge.

STEP 13

Again, add barriers on either side of the plate brick to keep cars where they belong. To give the bridge midsection something to rest on so that it won't fall when closed, attach a plate brick to the end of this section with a flat tile brick attached (as shown). This will hold the bridge in place until it is lifted again.

STEP 14

For some finer details, I created lampposts to run along the bridge. You can use antenna bricks with light and "final" bricks attached to the top. For the midsection, create smaller lamps using 1x1 bricks and light bricks on top.

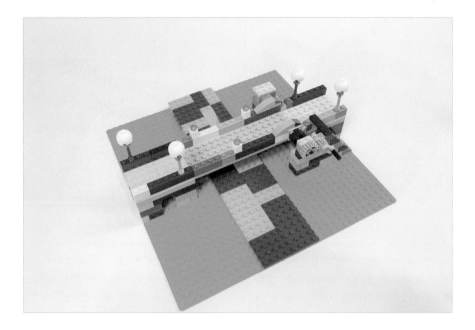

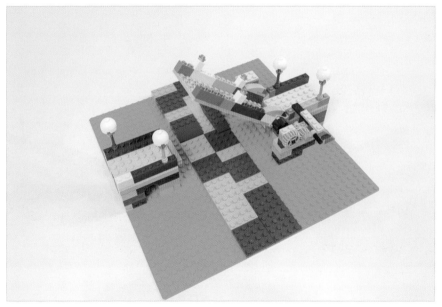

STEP 15

Finally, check that the bridge draws smoothly and rests closed firmly. When you're satisfied, send the cars and people over.

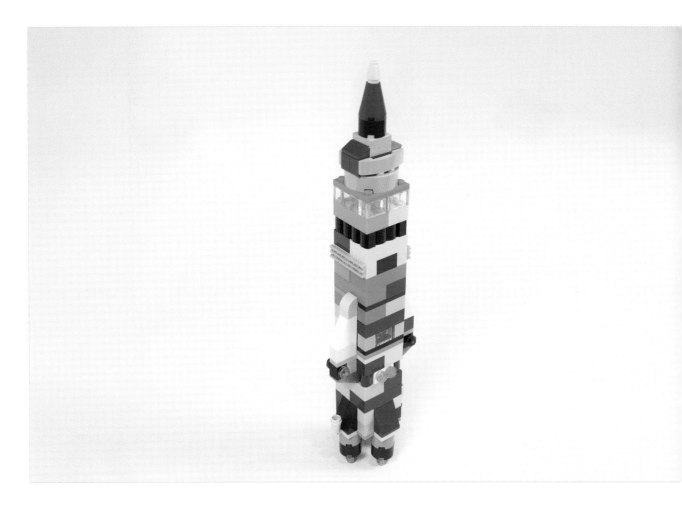

Space Rocket

Specialty pieces needed:

- Radiator grille bricks
- Palisade bricks
- Large cone
- 1x4 plate bow bricks

I have loads of fond memories of visiting the Kennedy Space Center as a kid, and I built my first ever LEGO spaceship when I returned home. This space rocket build is a little fancier, but will spark your children's imaginations just as much. With all its different parts, you can get your whole family involved in the build. When you're done, why not hang the spaceship from your kid's bedroom ceiling?

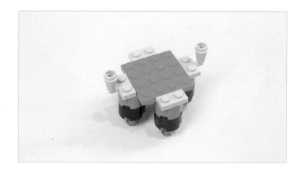

STEP 1

Find a 4x4 plate brick and flip it over. Stack four sets of 2x2 round bricks two high (as shown) for the propulsion rockets. They will need to poke out off the sides of the baseplate in order to fit. Attach orange light cone bricks onto the ends of the round bricks for the exhaust.

STEP 2

Flip this section back over, and then attach some 1x2 bricks onto the parts of the round bricks that are poking out to make this section level. I also added some plate bricks with a shaft and cone brick attached, but they're purely decorative to make the rocket look even more impressive!

STEP 3

Finish off this section of the rocket using roof tile bricks and regular bricks to bring the base together, making it 4x4 in size.

STEP 4

Add a couple of layers of regular bricks then attach a few more decorative bricks on top of this. I used 1x1 round bricks and knob bricks with lights on. On this level, also attach a 1x3 inverted roof tile brick on either side of the rocket to form the base of the rocket's wings.

STEP 5

Continue to build the rocket upwards, ensuring you build the wings up as well. Again, why not add decorative bricks, such as light bricks to make the rocket look even better?

STEP 6

When you get to the top of the wings, place a tall roof tile brick on top of each wing to make them more aerodynamic. Then use 1x1x1 arch bricks to fix the roof tile bricks into place at the top of the wings.

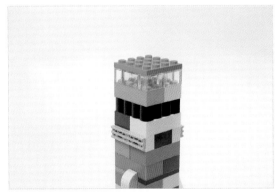

STEP 7

Add more layers of bricks above the wings to make the rocket really tall. At this stage, I attached radiator grille pieces to knob bricks, used palisade bricks and see-through bricks to add more cool details to the rocket. Customize yours to suit your space travel needs.

STEP 8

When your rocket has the height it needs, make the aerodynamic cone for the top. To begin, place a 4x4 plate brick at the top, then attach "inside and out bow" bricks to create a round section.

STEP 9

On top of the round section, add two rows of 1x4 knob bricks. Onto each, attach a 1x4 "plate bow" brick on the sides and small tile bricks on top (as shown).

STEP 10

Finally, create the tip of the nose cone by placing a 2x2 brick between the small tile bricks and attaching a large cone brick with a small cone brick on top. You're ready for launch!

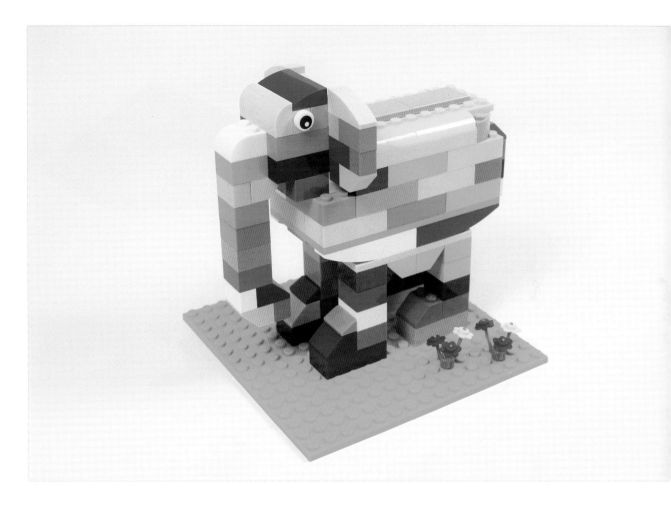

Elephant

Specialty pieces needed:

- 4 1x6 reverse bow bricks
- Flowers
- Eyes

When my wife and I went on our honeymoon to South Africa, we had the best experience walking with elephants in the wild, which is why it wasn't long until I was building one from LEGO with our little one.

This elephant build looks best when you use lots of brick colors. It includes all the things kids know and love about elephants: big ears, a long trunk, and big stompy feet!

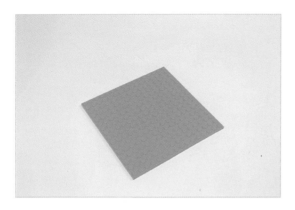 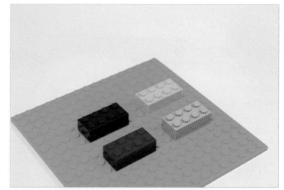

STEP 1

Find a 16x16 baseplate, and then place four 2x4 bricks on the baseplate for the base of the feet.

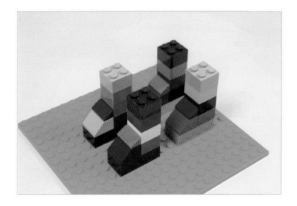

STEP 2

Use 2x2 bricks to build the elephant's legs up from the feet. Also use roof tile bricks at the front of the feet to give a more curved look, common to elephants.

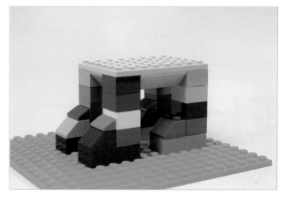

STEP 3

To start the body, place a 6x8 plate brick on top of the legs, and then attach inverted roof tile bricks angled outward to the underside of the plate brick, between each of the legs. This will give a rounded look to the elephant's belly.

STEP 4

To continue the rounded look, use inverted roof tile bricks and 1x6 reverse bow bricks at the front and back of the elephant. You can then place another plate brick on top of these if you like to make it easier to build on.

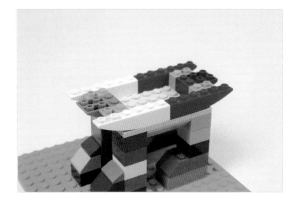

STEP 5

Use regular bricks to build up the side of the elephant. Be sure to add an inverted roof tile brick at the rump for later attaching the elephant's tail. Also, leave a space at the front of the elephant for attaching the head.

STEP 6

To create a curved look on top, attach rows of 4x1x1 bow bricks running along each side of the length of the elephant. Then at the back, use "inside and out bow" bricks with a regular brick in between to bring them together.

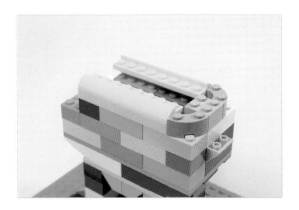

 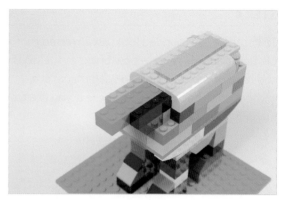

STEP 7

Connect the 4x1x1 bow bricks together with plate bricks, then run some flat tile bricks along the top of the elephant, and then begin building its neck. To do this, attach regular bricks of various sizes to the front and gradually build outwards from the elephant's body. Use a 2x6 brick for a trunk attachment.

STEP 8

On the long 2x6 brick, attach a 2x3 arch brick at the end. Then place a tile brick where the back of the head will go. For the eyes, attach 1x1 knob bricks to either side of the head with eye pieces attached.

STEP 9

To finish off the elephant's head, attach a 1x4 1/3 curved brick and 2x4 plate bow brick on top. Then for the ears, attach a 1x1x1 arch brick towards the back on either side of the head. It's these bricks that will keep the ears in place.

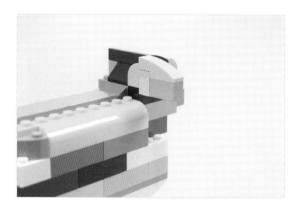 

STEP 10

To the 1x1x1 arch bricks, attach some 1x3 bow bricks then use x1 wide regular and inverted roof tile bricks to construct the rest of the ears.

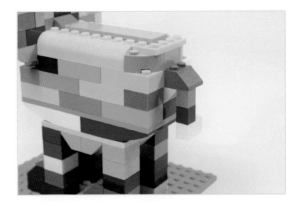

STEP 11

For the tail, attach a tile brick to the inverted roof tile brick that's poking out at the back. Then attach 1x1 bricks with a 1x2 brick at the bottom.

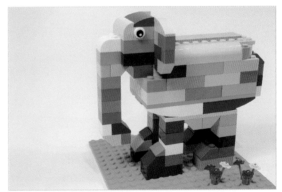

STEP 12

Finally, it's time to attach the elephant's trunk. Simply attach 2x2 bricks to the nose, which is poking out at the front. Then at the bottom of the trunk, use some roof tile and inverted roof tile bricks to give it some curvature. Now all your elephant needs is a name.

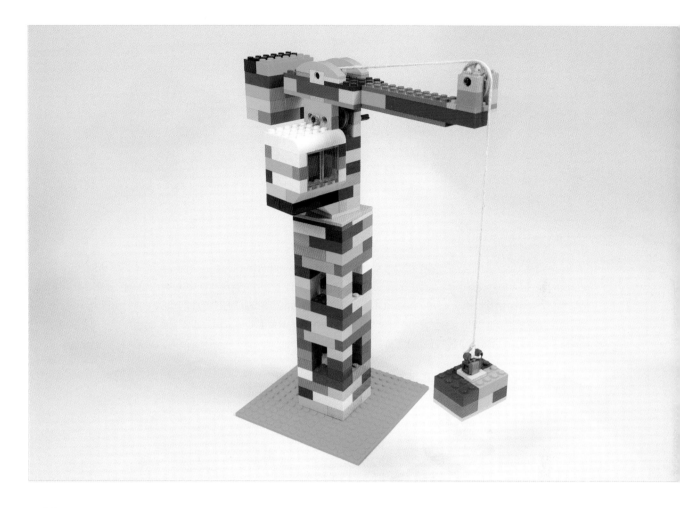

Crane

Specialty pieces needed:

- 2 1x4 bricks with 3 holes in
- 4 1x2 bricks with 1 hole in
- Medium length axle
- 2 short axles

- Axle handle
- 2x4 plate brick with 3 holes in
- 5 ½ bushes for axles
- Bush for axle

- 2 wedge belt wheels
- String

Sometimes bigger is better! This crane build is brilliant if you want something that moves and stands tall. The crane has an operator's cab attached to the side, just like on the ones you see in the city. Plus, it includes a pulley mechanism so the crane can easily lift and drop items at the turn of its hand crank.

Besides offering another great introduction to basic mechanics for your kids, the crane also teaches the concept of balance as it requires a counterweight for it to remain stable and balanced when carrying a weight. Your kids will have lots of problem-solving practice not only during the build, but also while trying to find ways for the crane to work how they want it to.

STEP 1

If you're building your crane on a hard surface, find a 16x16 plate brick for the crane to sit on. If on carpet, build the crane on a large baseplate, ensuring the entire crane structure sits within the confides of the baseplate. Once you've chosen a suitable base, start building the tall mast that the boom and counterweight will balance from at the top. Remember, the taller you make the crane, the wider the mast should be to ensure it remains stable.

STEP 2

Use regular bricks to build the mast, ensuring the bricks are staggered so they always overlap each other. When you're happy with the height of the mast, place plate bricks on top.

 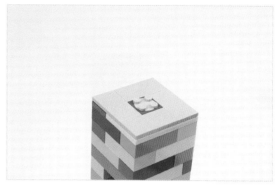

STEP 3

In the middle of the mast attach a turning plate, then fix 2x4 flat tile bricks around the turning plate. This will allow the section at the top of the mast to rotate freely and easily without getting stuck.

STEP 4

Now we'll construct the top, rotatable section of the crane, which includes the cab, boom, and counterweight. First, attach a 4x4 plate brick onto the turning plate, and then add a layer of regular bricks with some inverted roof tile bricks on one side.

STEP 5

On the next layer, use long, 2x6 bricks to create a section that sticks out on one side to support the crane's cab.

STEP 6

For the crane operator's cab, attach inverted roof tile bricks at the front to give the operator a clearer view of the crane when it's at work. At the same time, continue to build up the mast on this section, to the right of the cab.

STEP 7

Attach some window bricks to the cab's front on the inverted roof tile bricks and use 2x3 arch bricks to form the roof of the cab. Use x1 wide bricks for the side and back of the cab.

STEP 8

Next we'll create the mechanism to pull the string up and down. Attach a 1x4 brick with 3 holes in onto the edge of the mast as shown, ensuring it's attached to a brick that's x1 wide. Into the middle hole, insert a medium-length axle and place a ½ bush then handle on the end. Ensure the axle extends over the cab's roof.

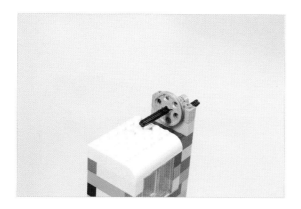

STEP 9

Place a wedge belt wheel onto the axle so it sits on the opposite side of the brick from the handle. You'll tie the string to this piece later. Attach another 1x4 brick with 3 holes in to the top of the cab, threading the axle through it, and secure this end of the axle in place using ½ bush.

STEP 10

Add 1x4 bricks above the bricks with holes, and then place a 2x4 plate brick with 3 holes across these, directly above the axle. The string will pass through these holes. Next, attach two 4x4 plate bricks to either side.

STEP 11

Attach a row of x1 wide bricks along both long edges of the plate bricks section, then attach a couple of long x2 wide bricks to the front for the boom section. You'll need to secure the pieces together using plate bricks underneath. For the rear section, attach a 2x6 brick to later hold the counterweight. Make sure the plate brick with holes remains uncovered.

STEP 12

Use more x2 wide and 4x4 plate bricks on top of this section to further secure all the parts into place.

STEP 13

To attach the counterweight, put together a block of regular bricks and attach them to the brick that's poking out from the back of the crane. This counterweight will keep the crane balanced when it's lifting things.

STEP 14

Above the first axle, slide a bush piece (with a ½ bush either side) onto a short axle. Secure into place using a couple of 1x2 bricks with 1 hole in. Secure this section down with 1x3 bow bricks and plate bricks to make sure it stays in place when the crane is lifting. This section will allow the string to travel all the way to the end of the boom.

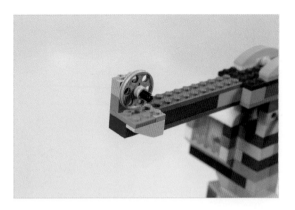 

STEP 15

Now slide a wedge belt wheel and ½ bush onto a short axle. Attach to the end of the boom using two 1x2 bricks with 1 hole in. This part will allow the string to freely move from the boom to the bottom of the crane. Give the wheel a spin to test if it moves freely.

STEP 16

We're ready to thread the lifting cable. Cut a length of string that is longer than the length of the boom plus the height of the mast; you need some excess to tie it in place, after all.

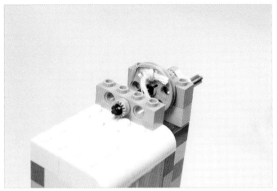

STEP 17

To attach the string, remove the boom and counterweight section from above the cab, and then tie one end of the string to the wedge belt wheel.

STEP 18

Feed the string up through the 2x4 plate brick with 3 holes in on the boom and counterweight section, and then fix the section back into place.

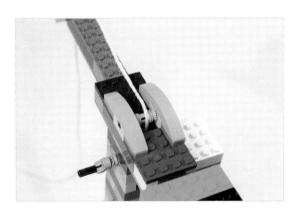

STEP 19

Run the string over the bush piece and then over to the wedge belt wheel at the end of the boom.

STEP 20

The end of the string needs a device to attach to the items to be lifted. You can create one in many ways, but here I attached a 2x2 knob plate brick to a 1x1 knob brick with a loop piece attached either side. You can easily attach this hook to the top of other LEGO bricks to be lifted.

STEP 21

Tie the string from the crane onto each of the loop bricks (or in the way that works best for your hook device). To lift something, simply rotate the top section of the crane to line it up and attach the hook to your container. Then use the hand-crank at the top to wind the string up to lift it.

Car Carrier Trailer

Specialty pieces needed:

- Short axle
- Windshield

Soon after my son's car obsession, he turned his focus onto trucks—so I think it's fairly obvious where the inspiration for this build came from! This car carrier features a separate truck and two-story trailer that holds a vehicle on each level. What's more, the top level folds down and the rear support converts into a ramp, allowing cars to easily drive on.

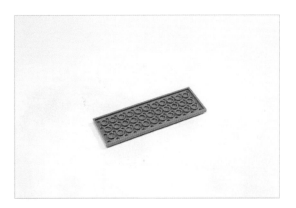

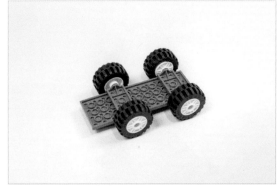

STEP 1

The truck that pulls the car trailer is relatively simple. To begin, find a 4x12, rectangular plate brick.

STEP 2

Flip the baseplate upside down, attach two-wheel suspension bricks, clip on wheel rims, and slip on some large, rugged tires.

STEP 3

At the front of the truck, attach a 1x4 knob brick and some radiator grille pieces. Then, add a layer of regular bricks onto the base of the truck.

STEP 4

Attach a 4x4 round brick that has a hole in the middle to the rear of the truck as a connection point for the trailer, and then add a 6x8 plate brick to the front end of the truck.

STEP 5

Add some more bricks on top of the plate brick, including some 1x1 knob bricks with light bricks for the truck's headlights. Also, use "inside and out bow" bricks at the front for the base of the cab.

STEP 6

Use windshield and window bricks to complete the cab's front and sides, and then use plate bricks for the roof. On top of the roof, add a 3x4 roof tile brick at the front for a wind deflector. Also attach a 2x2 round brick towards the back of the roof for the exhaust.

STEP 7

With the truck ready to haul, we will build the car trailer. Find a 6x16 rectangular plate brick that's the same width as the truck. Flip it over, and add a row of regular bricks to the underside, which the wheels will later sit on.

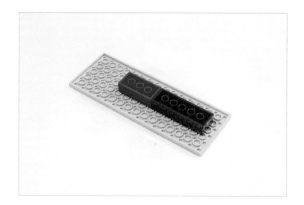

STEP 8

We now need to attach the hinges for the ramp at the rear of the trailer. To do this, place two plate bricks that have vertical forks on them at the back of the trailer and secure these into place with inverted roof tile bricks and plate bricks.

STEP 9

Now attach two sets of smaller wheels towards the back of the trailer using 1x4 bearing plate bricks. Secure them into place using a plate brick, and use inverted roof tile bricks around the wheel section to create a wheel arch.

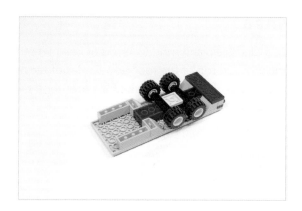

STEP 10

Attach a 2x6 regular brick to the underside, ensuring it pokes out from the front of the trailer. Secure it into place using plate bricks. This is what will connect the trailer to the truck.

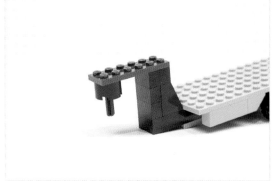

STEP 11

To make the coupler on the trailer level with the one on the truck, use regular and tall roof tile bricks to build on top of the brick poking out from the front of the trailer. Then add a 2x6 plate brick on top, attach a 2x2 round brick underneath it at the end, and insert a short axle inside the round brick. When you're ready to connect the truck and trailer, this axle will slot into the hole of the 4x4 round brick at the back of the truck.

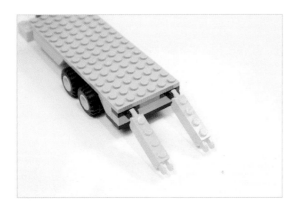
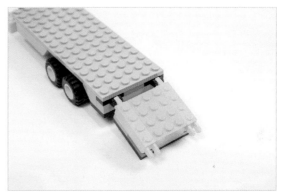

STEP 12

Next, attach the ramp to the back of the trailer: Attach a fork brick to each of the plate bricks with the forks that we attached in step 8. Connect the fork bricks together using plate bricks, with regular bricks in between to make the ramp level.

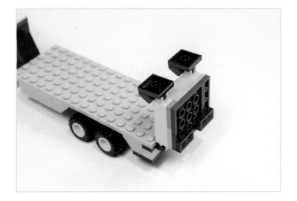
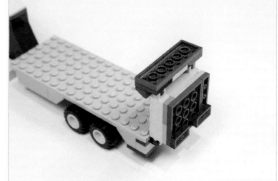

STEP 13

On the end of each fork brick, attach a 2x2 plate combi brick. Then attach the two combi bricks together using a 2x6 plate brick. This will hold the upper section of the trailer in place when the ramp is stowed, and it'll also be part of the ramp when unfolded.

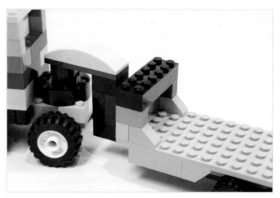

STEP 14

Next, fix the trailer to the back of the truck, checking that it's level and making any adjustments if needed. Now you're ready to start building the frame for the upper section of the trailer. At the front of the trailer, stack x1 wide bricks on each side and connect them with a 2x6 brick to help keep the structure secure as shown.

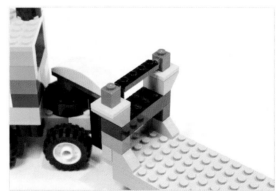

STEP 15

When you're happy with the height of the upper section, place a 2x2 nob plate brick with a 1x1 nob brick attached on either side of the structure. Attach a 1x4 bearing plate brick to each knob brick to act as a hinge so the top deck of the trailer can lower for cars to drive on.

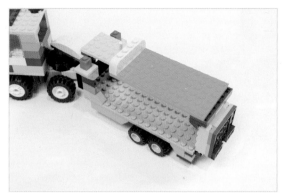

STEP 16

To build the top deck, attach a couple of large plate bricks together so this section reaches the ramp at the other end of the trailer when it's folded up. In addition, install a barrier at the front of the top deck using 1x1x1 arch bricks and plate bricks, to ensure cars can't roll forward.

STEP 17

So cars don't fall off, the trailer needs narrow barriers on either side. Do this by inserting antenna bricks into 1x1 knob bricks and fixing them into place on each side of both decks of the trailer. You can also add any other details, such as beacons.

STEP 18

Finally, build a couple of simple LEGO cars that will fit onto your car trailer. These can be really simply built using just a few bricks and wheels. Your car carrier truck and trailer are ready to hit the road.

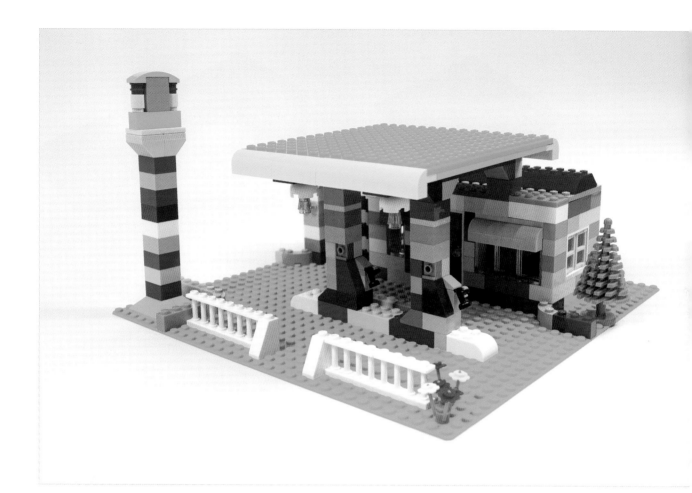

Gas Station

Specialty pieces needed:

- Tree
- Flowers
- Fencing
- Doors and windows
- 2x2 round bricks

When I was a kid, I was the proud owner of a LEGO Octan Gas Station. It was one of my favorite LEGO City buildings, because it had a working car wash, gas pumps, and loads of brilliant little features. Although it's now retired, that station inspired me to build one from scratch with my son. As you'll see, this station has a few good parts too, including a kiosk, a car wash, gas pumps, a forecourt roof, and a big gas station sign.

You can also build your own cars and gas tankers to go with it—or drive your car carrier by to fill up!

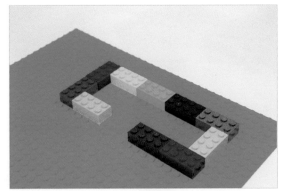

STEP 1

Find a large baseplate and lay the foundation for the gas station kiosk. Lay down regular bricks for the kiosk building in one corner of the baseplate.

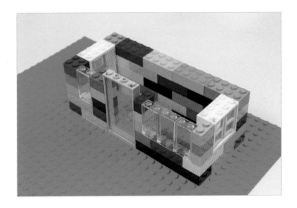
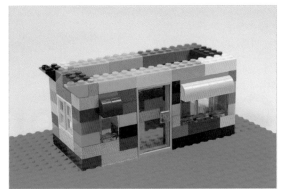

STEP 2

Be sure to include a door at the front with plenty of windows. I've also used 1x1x1 arch bricks above the windows for a small canopy. Continue building the walls up until you have one layer of bricks above the door. On the left corners of the kiosk, be sure to include a couple of inverted roof tile bricks. You'll connect the car wash structure to these in a few steps.

STEP 3

Next we'll start building the car wash section to the left of the kiosk. Build the far wall of the car wash, leaving at least six stubs between it and the kiosk.

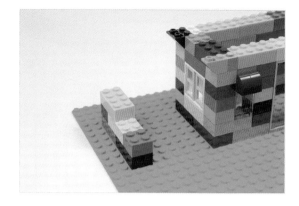

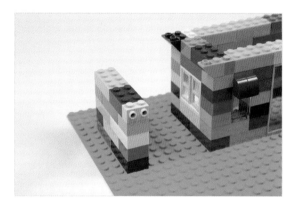

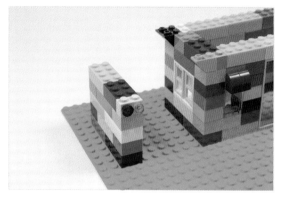

STEP 4

Halfway up this wall include a 1x2 double knob brick facing outward. Attach a red and a green light brick, so cars know when they can enter the car wash.

STEP 5

Finish building the car wash wall, again including inverted roof tile bricks at the top corners pointing towards the kiosk. Then place two 1x1 round bricks at the base of the entrance for the car wash brushes to sit on.

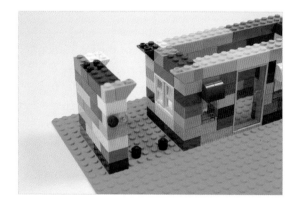

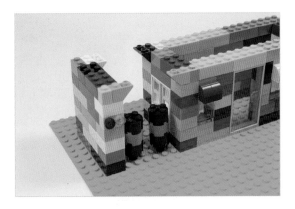
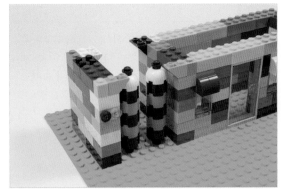

STEP 6

For each of the two brushes, stack up 2x2 round bricks then place a "final" brick with a 1x1 round brick on top. Remember to alternate the color of the round bricks if possible to make it look even more realistic.

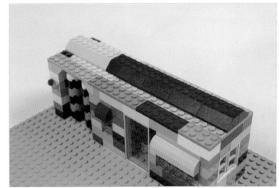

STEP 7

Use plate bricks to create a flat roof that covers the entire kiosk and car wash, and then run two rows of roof tile bricks along the length of the building.

STEP 8

Next, we'll build the section of the gas station that supports the forecourt roof and houses the gas pumps. Lay down a row of regular bricks between the kiosk and edge of the baseplate and place a 2x3 arch brick at each end of the row.

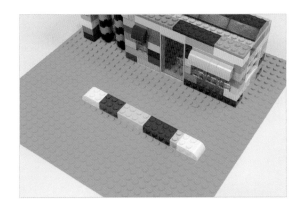

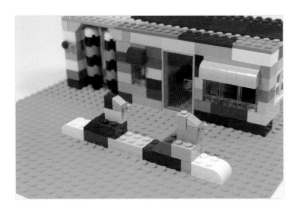
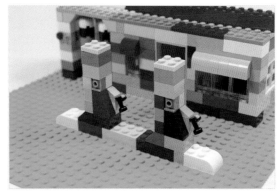

STEP 9

Use a variety of bricks to build the two gas pumps. For instance, I used roof tile, 1x1, clip, knob, and tap bricks. Once you're happy with how the pumps look, you'll need to ensure you can support pillars on top of them that are 2x2 in size (as shown). Add a couple of layers of 2x2 regular bricks then place one 2x2 plate brick on top of each pillar to make them level with the kiosk.

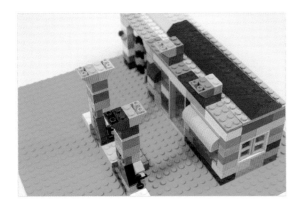
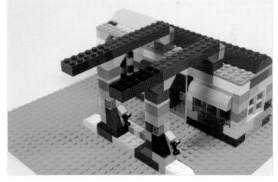

STEP 10

On top of each pillar add two inverted roof tile bricks. Also place inverted roof tile bricks on the roof of the kiosk, in line with the ones on top of the pillars.

STEP 11

Using long x2 wide regular bricks, attach beams reaching across from the kiosk to the pillars. Then use shorter bricks that reach out from the pillars so the rest of the forecourt can be covered.

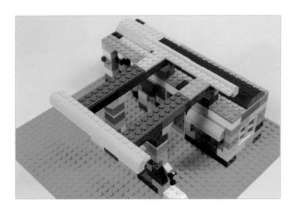 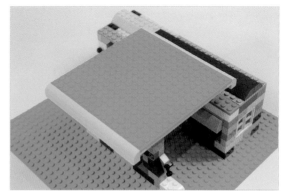

STEP 12

Secure the beams in place by attaching plate bricks on top. Then attach rows of 4x1x1 bow bricks across the ends of the beams as shown. Now top the whole assembly off with a 16x16 plate brick to finish the roof. This plate brick will also secure the bow bricks into place.

 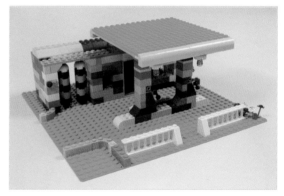

STEP 13

On the underside of the forecourt roof, add some lights. You can do this simply by attaching small orange cone bricks to the underside of "final" bricks, then attaching them to the underside of the roof.

STEP 14

Add some barriers around the gas station so cars know where they can drive. I used a variety of fence, "inside and out bow," and x1 wide bricks. Also make space at the corner of the forecourt for a gas station sign.

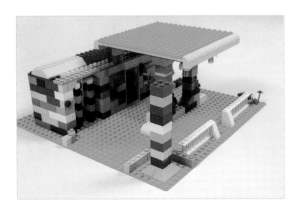
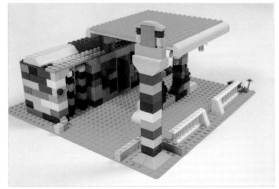

STEP 15

For the sign, build the base using four corner roof tile bricks then add a number of layers of 2x2 bricks on top. Then use whichever bricks you like to make a big colorful sign to sit on top of the tall column.

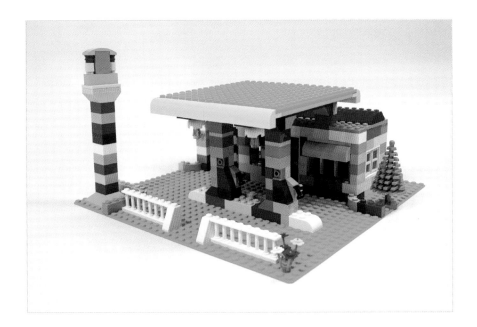

STEP 16

Finally, add any other embellishments to make your gas station come to life, then you're open for business.

FAMILY SPOTLIGHT

Parent: Mike Spee
Location: Kirkland, WA
Kid: Hunter, age 3

What are your favorite projects to build with your kid?
Hunter and I love to build things from her favorite shows (such as these builds from *Paw Patrol*).

What do you enjoy most about building with your child?
I love watching her creativity blossom and her confidence grow as she continues to build more.

What do they get most excited about when building?
Hunter loves creating games and activities out of her builds.

Do you usually keep your models/projects together or break them down afterwards?
We try to find a healthy balance so we don't run out of good pieces, though these *Paw Patrol* models have lasted quite a while!

Do you and/or your kids have a dream LEGO project they'd like to build?
This keeps changing, with new ideas coming all the time, but we look forward to many epic builds in our future!

6

LEGO in Motion

Since I got my first LEGO motor, LEGO builds that move are by far my favorite type to construct. This chapter showcases my all-time favorite LEGO pieces that involve the use of a motor or motion generated by hand. For example, I'll show you how to build a LEGO cable car, which was the first thing I built with my dad, as well as a helicopter, wind turbine, clock, and more. These projects are all brilliant to teach your kids the basics behind gears and general mechanics. The sky's the limit with some of these ideas. Don't be afraid to make your versions of these moving LEGO masterpieces big and bold!

Helicopter

Specialty pieces needed:

- 4 1x2 bricks with 1 hole in
- 2 small axles
- Long axle
- 3 medium gears

- Bush piece
- ½ bush piece
- Tiny gear
- 2x4 plate brick with 3 holes in

- Propeller
- Windshield
- Steering wheel
- Seat

As someone who loves aviation, I frequently built airplanes and helicopters when I was a kid. As my stock of LEGO increased and I began to inherit LEGO Technic bricks, such as gears and axles, I created this helicopter build. Not only do its blades spin around when you push the helicopter, it is a brilliant introductory build to help your kids learn the basics around how gears work. My next challenge is to construct a Chinook-style helicopter with two sets of rotor blades, using the same principles—but one step at a time!

STEP 1

Find a 4x12 plate brick, and then attach a 1x6 brick to each long edge on one end.

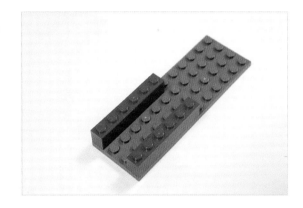

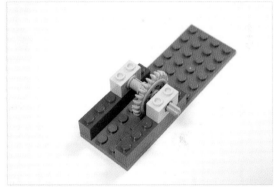

STEP 2

On top of each of these bricks, attach a 1x2 brick with 1 hole in, and then feed a short axle through the hole. Onto this axle, attach a medium-sized gear between the bricks, aligning it up against the right brick with 1 hole in. Ensure it's secured into place, using a bush piece on the inside.

STEP 3

On the right side, push the axle out and attach a medium-sized gear on the outside as well.

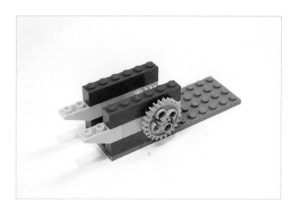 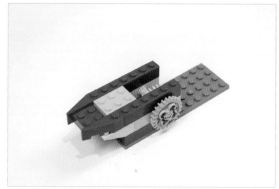

STEP 4

Now begin building up the rear of the helicopter, using x1 wide bricks and inverted roof tile bricks that will eventually lead to the tail section, where I've added an 18° 4x4 brick.

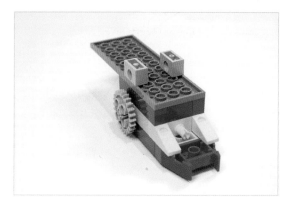 

STEP 5

Turn the helicopter upside down to attach a set of wheels, which will drive the mechanism that will spin the blades. Attach two 1x2 bricks with 1 hole in (as shown) then feed a long axle between them.

STEP 6

On the side of the helicopter that already has a gear sticking out, attach a suitably sized gear to the wheel axle that will ensure both gears make contact. Then attach a wheel onto each end of the axle on the underside of the helicopter (as shown). The wheel needs to be bigger than the gear that it's sharing an axle with to ensure it's only the wheels making contact with the ground and not the gear.

STEP 7

Now attach a single wheel to the front of the helicopter and any other details you like for the underside as well.

STEP 8

Flip the helicopter back over, and ensure it balances on the three wheels. Next, begin building the cockpit section of the helicopter using regular bricks and inverted roof tile bricks.

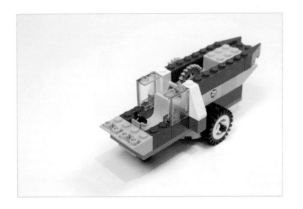 

STEP 9

Add window pieces and a windshield, so your pilot has a good view, as well as a seat and steering wheel brick, if you have them.

STEP 10

Next we need to construct the mechanism that will connect the driving gear to the helicopter blades. To do this, feed a small axle through the middle of a 2x4 plate brick with 3 holes in. On one end of the axle, attach a tiny gear (this will connect with the vertical gear inside the helicopter), and on the other end of the axle attach a ½ bush to keep everything in place.

STEP 11

Fix this section into place on top of 1x2 plate bricks above the vertical gear inside the helicopter. You'll probably have to make some minor adjustments to ensure all the gears connect. Test that this axle spins by rolling the helicopter forward.

STEP 12

Now add plate bricks on top of the helicopter to finish off the roof. I also attached some grille, light, 2x2 flat tile and 1x4 'plate bow' bricks to make it more realistic.

STEP 13

Attach a long x2 wide plate brick to the rear of the helicopter for its tail. Also attach a propeller to a 2x2 snap and cross brick to the end of the tail, along with a light brick for a beacon. Make sure this section isn't too long; otherwise your helicopter might fall backwards.

STEP 14

Construct the helicopter rotor blades by attaching four 1x8 plate bricks to a 2x2 round brick. Then place a "'final" brick on top, in the middle of the four blades.

STEP 15

Push the round brick on the underside of the blades onto the axle poking from the top of the helicopter, ensuring it can move freely. Push the helicopter forward to test that the blades spin, and then your helicopter is complete.

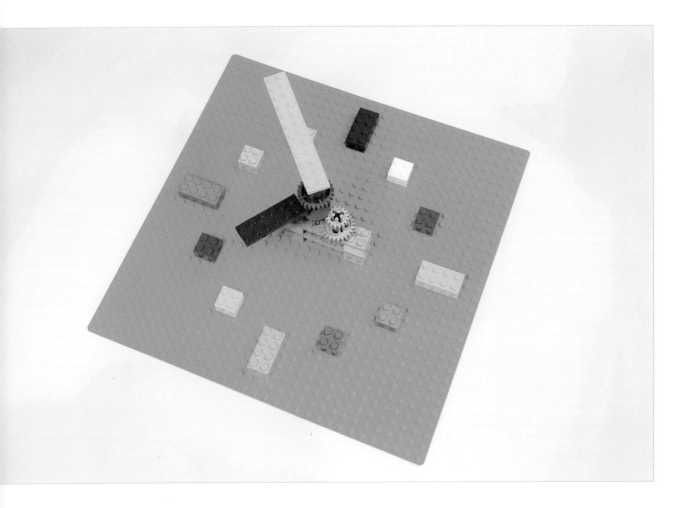

Crazy Clock

Specialty pieces needed:

- 2 2x8 plate bricks with 7 holes in
- Medium axle
- Long axle
- Medium gear
- Small gear
- Tiny gear
- ½ bush
- Differential gear

The Crazy Clock is a great educational build to demonstrate the basic workings of a clock. All of the mechanics are left exposed in this build, so your kids can see everything working when they spin the minute hand. The way the gears of varying sizes and shapes work together help to demonstrate how the minute and hour hand spin at different rates. Unfortunately, getting the hands to spin at exactly the right rate using LEGO pieces is pretty impossible (at least I haven't figured it out yet)! Therefore, this clock may show "crazy" times, and I wouldn't count on it to help you be on time for anything. When you do manage to display a correct time, why not turn it into a game where the kids have to guess what time is displayed? Made all the more fun by the fact the kids helped build the clock in the first place.

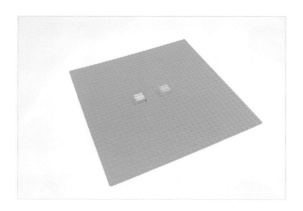
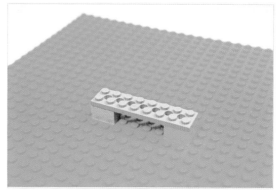

STEP 1

To a large baseplate, attach two 2x2 bricks in the middle with four studs between them. Add a 2x8 plate brick with 7 holes in across the top of them.

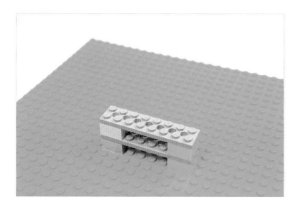
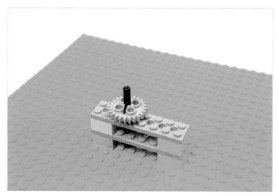

STEP 2

Stack another 2x2 brick on each end of the plate, and attach a second 2x8 plate brick with 7 holes in on top of these. This will help keep all the axles used in the clock mechanism steady.

STEP 3

Insert a medium axle through one of the holes on the left side of the plate brick. Choose one long enough to rest on the baseplate and leave enough space sticking up to hold two gears. Slide a medium gear onto the axle.

STEP 4

Insert a long axle through the hole to the right
the first axle. Thread a tiny gear onto this with a
½ bush on top, ensuring it makes contact with
the larger gear.

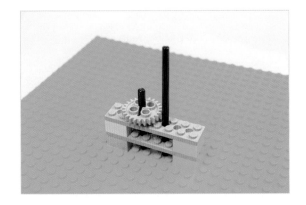

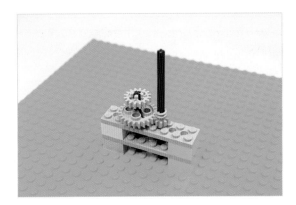

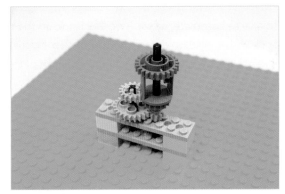

STEP 5

Insert a small gear onto the first axle above the medium gear, then insert a differential gear onto the
longer axle. Again, ensure the small gear and differential gear make contact. Notice the axle poking
through the top of the differential gear spins at a faster rate than the differential gear itself. This is
because the two axles in this build are spinning at different rates due to the difference in size of the
gears used. This LEGO differential gear is used in this way to mimic the shaft mechanism of a clock.

STEP 6

Next, place some bricks around the clock mechanism to symbolize the hours on a clock face. I
used longer bricks at 3, 6, 9, and 12 to make the
quarter hours more obvious.

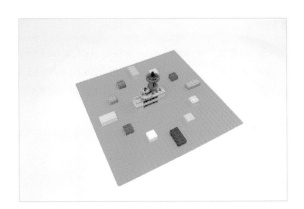

STEP 7

Now we'll construct the hour hand and attach it to the differential gear, which has a small attachment point inside. For the hour hand, therefore, attach a 1x6 plate brick under a 2x6 plate brick with one stud sticking out, and then attach a 1x1 clip brick to this. Attach this clip to the attachment point on the differential gear.

STEP 8

For the minute hand, attach a 2x2 round brick to the axle that's poking through the top of the differential gear. Attach a longer, 2x12 plate brick onto the round brick, and then your clock is complete. Simply turn the minute hand to see the basic workings of a clock in action.

Playground Swing

Specialty pieces needed:

- Long axle
- 2 bush pieces
- 2 1x2 bricks with 1 hole in

- 2 1x2 plate knob bricks
- Minifigure

- Flowers, wheelbarrow, other optional decor

My family loves going to our local park to spend as much time outdoors as possible on the swings and slides. It's not much fun in the pouring rain or on cold winter days, however, which inspired my son and me to build an indoor playground with LEGO.

This playground swing is a simple build that doesn't require many bricks. It's also the perfect starting point to build a full-blown playground. When you finish this build, put your imagination to work. From swings to roundabouts to seesaws, there are loads of moving things at the playground that you can build with LEGO.

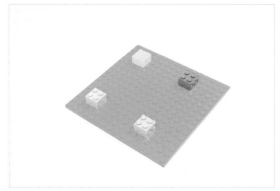

STEP 1

On a 16x16 baseplate, use 2x2 regular bricks that are 8 studs apart along the length, and 6 studs apart along the width, to build up the four pillars of your playground swing.

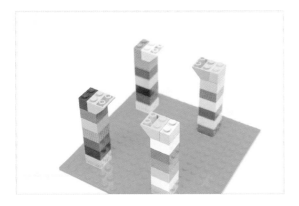
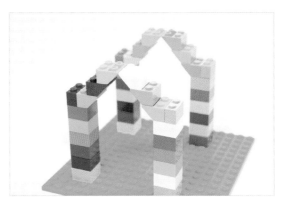

STEP 2

When you've made the swing 6 bricks high, begin using inverted roof tile bricks to bring the pillars together until they come to a point and meet in the middle.

STEP 3

Then use regular roof tile bricks on the outer side of the pillars to make them stronger and give a finished, sloping look.

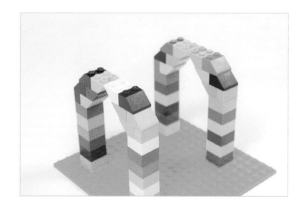

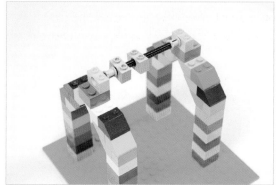

STEP 4

We now need to bridge the gap between the two sides of the swing: Attach a 1x2 brick with 1 hole in to the top of each side of the swing, and insert a long axle between them. On the axle, slide a couple of 1x2 bricks with 1 hole in onto the axle (you'll later attach the swing seat to these), and slide on some bush pieces to keep the axle in place.

STEP 5

Next, attach some bricks around the axle section to secure it into place on each side of the swing. Here I use plate, roof tile and 1x4 "plate bow" bricks.

STEP 6

Now we'll build the swing seat. Find a plate brick that's big enough to fit a LEGO person on (I used a 2x6). On either short end, attach a 1x2 brick with a 1x2 plate knob brick on top.

STEP 7

On top of the plate knob bricks, add a few layers of 1x1 bricks. On top of these, place an antenna piece to act as the swing chains.

STEP 8

On top of each antenna piece, slide on a 1x1 knob brick with 2 knobs, sideways.

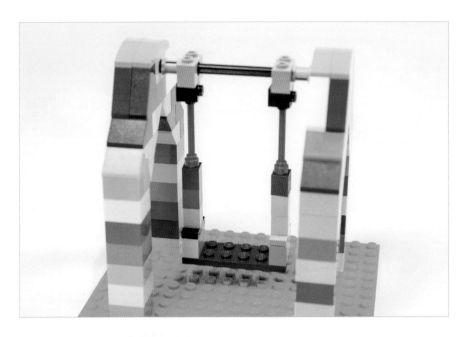

STEP 9

Attach the knob bricks to the underside of the 1x2 bricks with 1 hole in on the axle, so the seat swings freely. Finally, add any finer details around the swing and, of course, a little LEGO person on the seat to enjoy the swing!

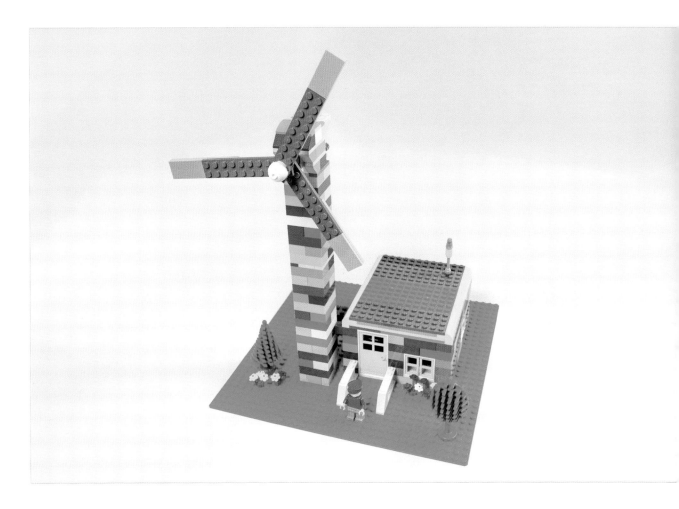

Wind Turbine

Specialty pieces needed:

- LEGO motor
- 2x4 basic brick with 3 holes in
- 2 2x4 plate bricks with 3 holes in
- 3 1x2 bricks with 1 hole in
- Medium axle
- 5 ½ bush pieces
- Small gear
- Tiny gear
- 4 long axles
- 2 axle connectors
- Medium gear
- Worm gear
- Flowers and trees

Not only are wind turbines becoming more and more common wherever you go, now more than ever they are playing such an important role in the impact we're having on the environment. Naturally, as my family loves building things from LEGO that either move or are big and impressive, the time came for us to build a wind turbine—it checks both the boxes! The build uses a LEGO motor to power the wind turbine blades from the base of the structure, making it a great demonstration of how you can transfer power from a motor over a long distance, as well.

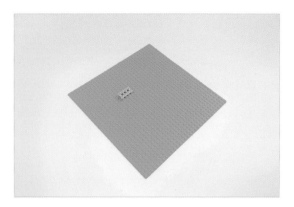
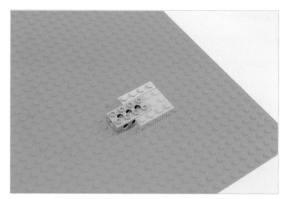

STEP 1

On a large baseplate, place a 2x4 brick with 3 holes in at the base of where you'd like the wind turbine to be built. This brick will anchor the axle that will drive power up to the wind turbine blades to make them spin. Around this brick, begin building the main wind turbine column, but leave one hole sticking out for the axle.

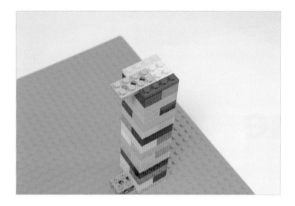

STEP 2

The axle will run up the outside of the column, so as you build it upwards be sure to add a 2x4 plate brick with 3 holes in that pokes out of the back in line with the 2x4 brick at the base. Because of the height of the wind turbine, the axle will be quite long and these bricks with holes will help keep it steady.

STEP 3

When you've built the column as tall as you'd like it, be sure to place a final 2x4 plate brick with 3 holes in at the top.

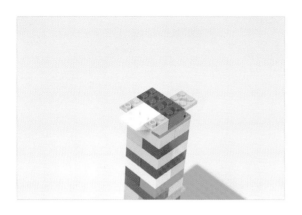

STEP 4

We now need to build the section where the turbine rotor blades will attach to the top of the column and to the drive axle. Start by building a platform for the blades to sit on. Set a 4x4 plate brick back from the edge by one stub and use inverted roof tile bricks to extend the platform out at the front, as shown.

STEP 5

On this platform, place a 1x2 brick with 1 hole in at the front and back. Insert a medium axle, and then attach a small gear above the 2x4 plate brick with 3 holes in (as shown). Use two ½ bush pieces to hold the axle in place.

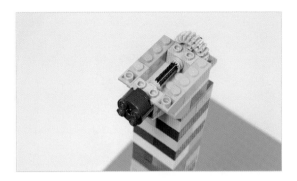 

STEP 6

On the front, push a 2x2 round brick onto the axle (you'll attach the turbine blades to this in the last step). Place plate bricks on top of the platform.

STEP 7

On top of the platform, attach a roof tile brick at the front to make this section aerodynamic, as well as an orange light brick at the back to act as a beacon. (I also added some decorative embellishments, such as 1x4 "plate bow" bricks.)

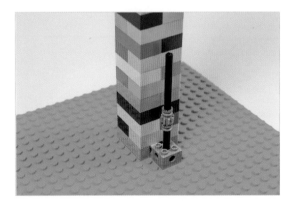 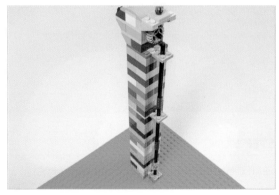

STEP 8

Next, we'll construct the axle that will drive power up the tall column to the wind turbine. Start by inserting a long axle into the brick with holes in on the baseplate, and slide a tiny gear onto the bottom of the axle so we can connect a motor. Keep this gear in place using 2 ½ bush pieces. Attach further long axles to this first one, threading them through the plate bricks with holes in, until the axle assembly reaches the top. Connect multiple axles together using axle connectors.

STEP 9

At the top, place a medium gear onto the axle that's driving up the column, ensuring it makes contact with the gear attached to the horizontal axle that'll have the rotor blades on.

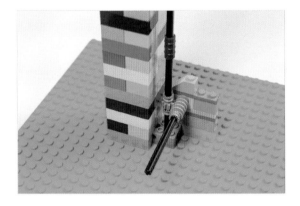
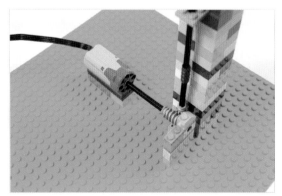

STEP 10

We now need to attach the LEGO motor. As the motor I'm using is quite fast, I used a worm gear to significantly slow its speed down, so the wind turbine doesn't spin too fast. Position an axle with a worm gear attached, horizontal to the vertical axle that runs up the windmill. Secure the worm gear into place with a ½ bush piece and ensure it makes contact with the tiny gear at the bottom. Fix the horizontal axle into place using a 1x2 brick with 1 hole in on top of x1 wide bricks, as shown. Attach the other end of the horizontal axle to your motor.

If you don't have a motor, simply attach a turning handle onto the axle with the worm gear on, instead of a motor.

STEP 11

With the motor securely in place, begin constructing a building next to the wind turbine to house the motor.

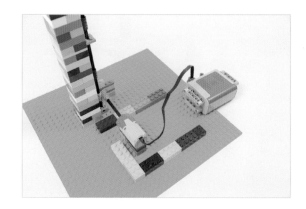

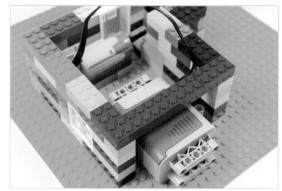

STEP 12

Leave space in one wall for the drive axle to run through and in the rear wall for the power box to fit into.

STEP 13

Securely attach the outbuilding to the wind turbine column. As there are moving parts attached between the two structures, ensuring they're fastened together will mean the mechanisms will stay securely in place.

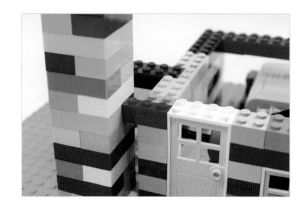

STEP 14

Finally, once the motor and battery box are completely concealed, attach 4x1x1 bow bricks and small plate bricks to the top, to form a roof.

STEP 15

Now it's time to construct the three turbine rotor blades. Attach x2 wide plate bricks together until the blades are as long as you want them. I added a 2x4 plate tile brick at the outer end of each one, too.

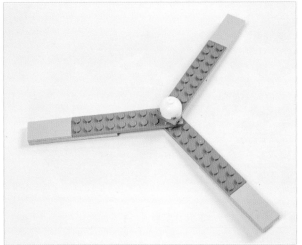

STEP 16

Attach the rotor blades to each other using a 1x1 round plate brick between the inner end of each blade (as shown). Separate the blades until they're all an equal distance apart from each other, then attach a "final" brick to the middle.

STEP 17

Finally, attach the turbine blades to the 2x2 round brick you added to the axle at the top of the column in step 6, and then add any finishing touches around the motor housing at the bottom of the wind turbine. Hit the power switch, and watch your wind turbine whirl away.

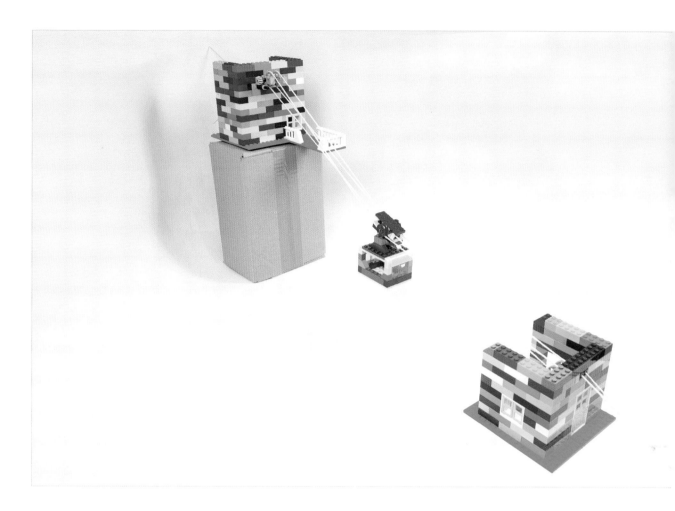

Cable Car

Specialty pieces needed:

- LEGO motor
- 2 long axles
- 3 medium axles
- 2x4 regular brick with 3 holes in
- 2 worm gears

- 2 medium gears
- 2 small gears
- 3 bush pieces
- 3 ½ bush pieces
- 2x4 plate brick with 3 holes in
- 6 1x2 bricks with 1 hole in

- 2 1x6 bricks with 5 holes in
- 2 1x4 bricks with 3 holes in
- 4 wedge belt wheels
- String

This is without doubt my all-time favorite LEGO build. As a kid, I remember coming back from a holiday in Cape Town, and I was desperate to build the cableway that travels up and down Table Mountain. Needless to say we weren't home long before I broke open my box of LEGO and got started recreating it with my dad. We even submitted a photo of it to the LEGO Club. I've made huge versions of this build, which have worked really well, so don't let size hold you back.

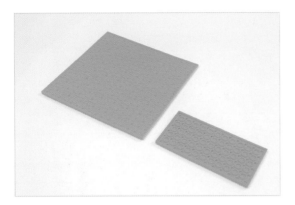 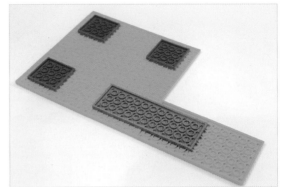

STEP 1

We'll start by making the top cable car station. Find a 16x16 plate brick for the station floor and attach a smaller, rectangular plate brick sticking out at the end to act as a platform for people to board and disembark the cable car. To level the floor, add square plate bricks underneath the 16x16 plate brick's other corners as shown.

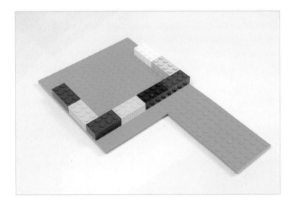 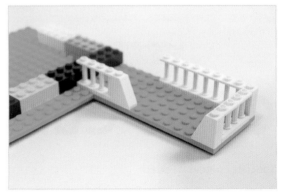

STEP 2

Begin building the front wall of the station. Also line the edges of the platform with fence bricks to make it safe.

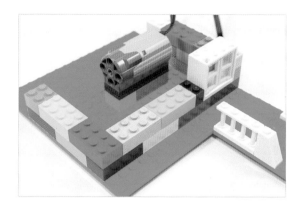

STEP 3

The motor to power the cableway will sit in this upper station, so ensure the walls leave enough room to then fit a LEGO motor in this section. There are various types of LEGO motors, fit yours in a way that it securely attaches to the 16x16 size plate brick.

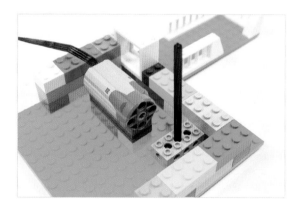

STEP 4

While building the walls of the station, keep in mind how you'll transfer power from the motor to the wedge belt wheels that will move the cable car. A worm gear will significantly slow down the speed of the motor to provide a nice comfy ride. Build this part by sliding a worm gear with a bush piece on either side of it onto a medium axle, then attach this to your motor. Then insert a long axle vertically into a 2x4 brick with 3 holes in—slide a medium gear onto this axle so it makes contact with the worm gear (or consult the instructions in Chapter 2).

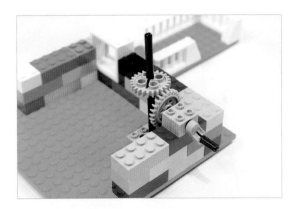

STEP 5

If you're not using a motor for propulsion, instead align two gears at right angles on axles (as shown), where the horizontal axle pokes through 1x2 bricks with 1 hole in, with a turning handle on the end. The 1x2 bricks with holes in should be on the wall of the upper cableway station, and I'd advise not to use a worm gear as it'll make the cable car move too slowly when using manual motion.

STEP 6

At the back of the station, add some 1x2 bricks with 1 hole in on either side. To keep the station in place while maintaining tension in the string, you'll tie the station down through these bricks so it doesn't topple over.

STEP 7

When the upper station is tall enough that the cable car will sit level with the boarding platform when the string is pulled taut, slide a small gear onto the vertical axle, secured into place with a 2x4 plate brick with 3 holes in, underneath the gear. Then slide a medium gear onto a long axle, secured into place with 2 1x2 bricks with 1 hole in, at a right angle to the small gear. Ensure the teeth of the two gears make contact. This is to bring a driving axle through to the front of the station, at a right angle to the front wall (as shown). Finally slide a worm gear onto this horizontal axle, secured into place with a bush and ½ bush piece. Refer to "Changing the direction of axles" in chapter 2 if you need help doing this.

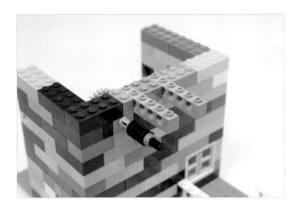 

STEP 8

Now use two 1x6 bricks with 5 holes in and have them poking out at the top. Insert a medium axle between these bricks, sliding two wedge belt wheels on the axle. Make sure there's space between them so the cables you'll string through them will remain separated. Attach a small gear, as shown, onto this axle to connect the driving axle to the wedge belt wheels via the worm gear.

 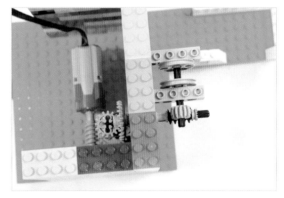

STEP 9

Build more layers of bricks above this section in order to secure the wedge belt wheels in place. This will ensure they don't detach under the tension of the string and weight of the cable car.

STEP 10

Finally, with the upper cable car station complete, place it on top of something tall (I used a cardboard box), and tie it down to a heavy object, e.g. the leg of a table it's standing on, or a pile of books, so it can't topple over.

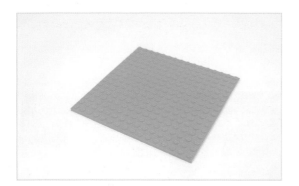

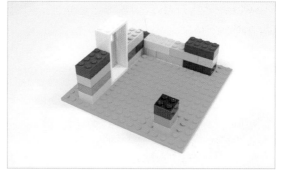

STEP 11

To build the lower cable car station, find a 16x16 plate brick and start constructing a three-walled building.

STEP 12

On one side, build an entrance so people can board the cable car when it arrives at the lower station.

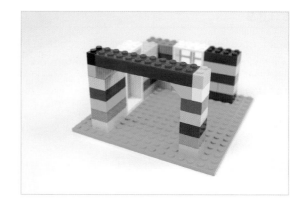

 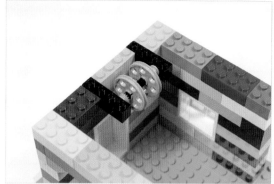

STEP 13

As you did for the top cable car station in step 8, add two 1x4 bricks with 3 holes in. This time, however, point them inside the building. Run a medium axle between them with two wedge belt wheels attached. Use two ½ bush pieces on the axle, between the wedge belt wheels and bricks with holes in, to stop it from sliding from side to side. Because the motor (or crank) is in the top station, these wedge belt wheels don't need to be connected to any gears, they can merely stand alone at the top rear of the bottom station.

 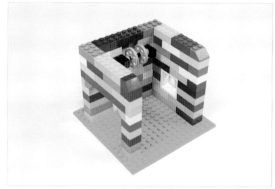

STEP 14

Add two 1x1 knob bricks to the back of this station too, again to tie it down so it doesn't move under the tension of the string. Plus, add some more layers of bricks above the wedge belt wheels to secure them into place for when the cableway is operating.

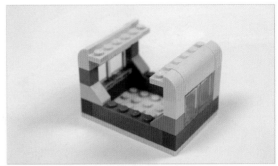

STEP 15

Next we'll build the cable car itself. Start with a 6x8 plate brick then use x1 wide bricks and window bricks to build the sides and front of the cable car. I used 4x1x1 bow bricks at either end of the cable car to give it a more authentic look.

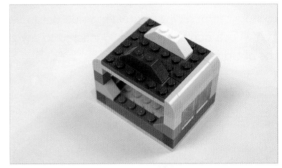

STEP 16

Add a roof to the cable car using plate bricks, and then use some narrow roof tile bricks to build the base of the support that will connect the cable car to the string.

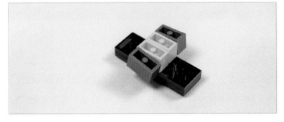

STEP 17

To help keep the cable car level (and passengers comfortable) while it's ascending and descending, we need to construct a leveling mechanism that will attach to its top. Find two 2x6 plate bricks, stacked on top of each other, and attach two 1x2 bricks with 1 hole in to the middle underside of the plate bricks. Now attach a 1x2 snap and cross brick to each of the bricks with holes in (as shown).

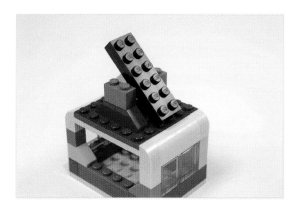
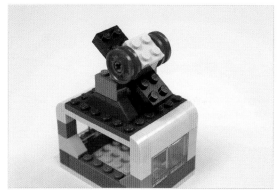

STEP 18

Attach this section to the supports you placed onto the cable car roof in step 16, then add a set of rims (without tires), connected by a snap and cross brick, to the top of the leveling mechanism.

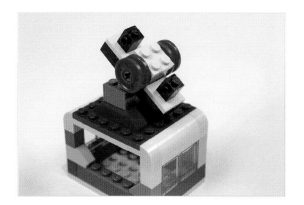

STEP 19

Attach a 1x1 knob brick (which has 2 knobs on) to either end of the leveling mechanism (you'll feed the string through these next), connected by a 2x2 plate knob brick. Then secure this section with a 2x6 plate brick on top.

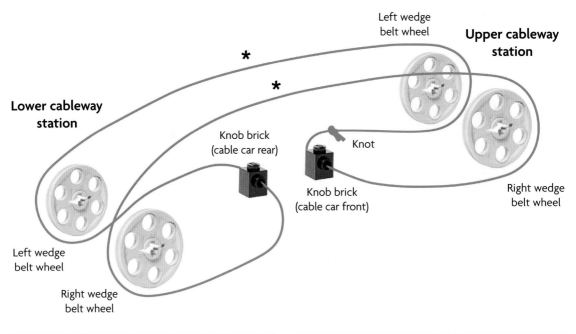

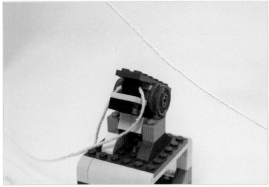

STEP 20

Cut a single piece of string that you'll need to feed through the wedge belt wheels of each station and through the knob bricks on the cable car. The piece of string needs to be 4 times longer than the length of your cableway, so I recommend making it 5 times longer to account for any wastage.

With the cable car sitting between the two stations, following the diagram, feed your string through the left knob of the knob brick on the front of the cable car. Then feed the string under then over the right wedge belt wheel on the top cableway station. Pull the string down to the bottom station then over and under the right wedge belt wheel. Feed the string through the right knob of the knob brick on the rear of the cable car, then pull the string back down to the bottom station and under then over the left wedge belt wheel. Draw the string up to the top cableway station, feeding it over and under the left wedge belt wheel.

Finally, the two ends of the string will meet. Tie the ends together next to the knob brick on the front of the cable car.

STEP 21

For the two lengths of string that connect between the two stations from the top of the wedge belt wheels (marked with an asterisk on the diagram), tuck these pieces of string underneath the wheel rims on top of the cable car.

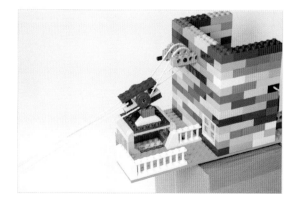

STEP 22

With the upper cable car station tied down, carefully pull the lower station away, putting tension on the string, which, in turn, will lift the cable car off the floor. Move the bottom station to a position where you think the tension will allow the cable car to sit level with the platform on the upper station when it arrives.

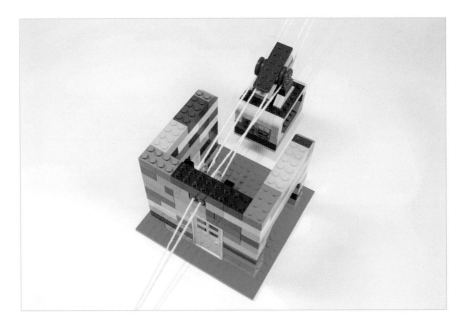

STEP 23

When you're satisfied with the position of everything, tie the bottom station down using string tied to the knob bricks at the back.

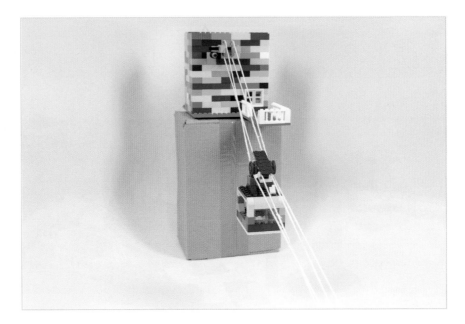

STEP 24

Finally, power up the motor (or start cranking) and watch your cable car move between stations. Make any tweaks in position once the cable car has done a few runs up and down, then enjoy playing with this awesome LEGO build.

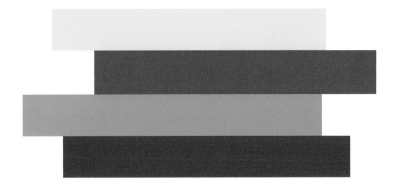

Conclusion

Well that's it, friends! I hope you've enjoyed exploring all the exciting things you can build with LEGO and found inspiration in the book's projects—not only for new builds but also for ways to get your family involved too. Remember, it's thinking outside the box that really makes LEGO the best toy ever. You don't have to be too prescriptive when following the steps in this book. If you don't have a brick featured in a build, simply find a close substitute or adapt the build to work with the bricks you do have. That's the beauty about LEGO: There's no right or wrong way. Plus, you may just come up with something even more fantastic by improvising!

From building games, gifts, things that move, or objects you've seen while out and about, the best LEGO builds always have a story behind them and have a purpose of bringing families together. All the builds in this book are special to me, whether because I used to build them growing up or because I build them with my son now that I'm a father. I hope you and your family create lifelong memories, just like I did, from the time you spend building together.

Nothing makes me happier than hearing stories and seeing photos from people who have made my creations at home. So please, if you and your family build anything from this book, share it on social media using the hashtag #LEGOWithDad. I can't wait to see your best LEGO creations!

Acknowledgments

I can't believe I'm actually able to say I have a book published about something that has had such a big influence in my life. If you had said to my eight-year-old self that I was going to author a book about all the great things I love to build with LEGO, I would have said that would be an absolute dream come true—yet here I am. It's happened! I may not have made it into the monthly *LEGO Club Magazine* as a kid (despite my best efforts), but now I can say I have my own book—just wow!

Since I started my journey with this publication, I have realized so much organization, planning, and creativity goes into putting a book together—something I never really appreciated before. Therefore, I owe so much to a host of people who helped me put this creation together.

Firstly, a huge thank you to Kelly Reed for believing in me and being so patient whilst I put together all the chapters of my book. In my naivety, I thought writing and photographing my first book would be absolutely no problem whilst being a parent, oh, and moving house at the same time. How wrong I was! So, thank you Kelly for bearing with me whilst I juggled everything to get the book where it is today.

Thanks also to my superstar manager, Craig Knox, who has kept me on the straight and narrow through the whole process. You've been a great source of knowledge, and you were always there to offer great advice whilst keeping me sane and laughing throughout.

For helping to bring the book to fruition and offering so much advice and expertise, a huge thanks to Linda Laflamme for doing such a thorough job at dotting the i's and crossing the t's. And to Aren Straiger for doing such a superb job in making the book look as vibrant and eye-catching as it is.

I wouldn't be where I am today without the support of the community on my YouTube channel. Thank you to everyone who has subscribed and continued to watch me on my journey creating video content. You've always supported me and provided constructive criticism, which has helped me no end to make my best content yet. If it weren't for you, I wouldn't be here writing my first book.

I love my Mom and Dad so much, and I'll be forever grateful to you for giving me the gift of LEGO from such a young age. I have so many fond family memories growing up playing with LEGO with you both; they really were some of the best years. Dad, I hope you're proud of where I've come so far, and Mom, I hope you're looking down, proud of your boy.

Finally, I am so unbelievably grateful to my wife Trisha. Since we met, you have been patient beyond belief with me and supportive with absolutely everything I do, no matter how absurd at times! You have supported me through all the working nights and all the stresses that come with it. Thank you so, so much.

And of course, thank you for bringing our pride and joy, Charlie, into our lives. We really are an awesome little team, and I couldn't imagine a moment without either of you. Charlie, you don't know it, but you've given me so much inspiration and drive to put this book together.

About the Author

Warren Nash started out as a YouTuber, creating content on DIY and food. Since the launch of his first channel, Warren has achieved over 15 million views with a huge following across the globe and garnered multiple awards. He has also presented on the BBC and worked with LEGO, T-fal, Audi, and top UK supermarkets, among other brands. Now a father, Warren has also seen success with a series of content based around fatherhood, arts and crafts, and other activities you can do with kids, as well as his series on the LEGO Family channel—warrennash.co.uk/legofamilychannel

Warren is keen to show parents fun ways to strengthen their bonds with their children with something that played such a big role in his life growing up: LEGO. Offering so many possibilities, LEGO has grown with him and constantly kept his imagination alive and creativity going. Now he wants to share his huge range of LEGO builds, which are perfect for people of all ages to build together.